STURGIS

Gerald Foster

Motorbooks International
Publishers & Wholesalers ®

First published in 1993 by Motorbooks International Publishers & Wholesalers, PO Box 2, 729 Prospect Avenue, Osceola, WI 54020 USA

Library of Congress Cataloging-in-Publication Data
Foster, Gerald.
    Sturgis: guide to the world's greatest motorcycle rally / Gerald Foster.
      p. cm.
    Includes index.
    ISBN 0-87938-735-1
    1. Motorcycle racing—South Dakota—Sturgis—Guidebooks. 2. Sturgis Region (S.D.)—Guidebooks. 3. Black Hills (S.D. and Wyo.)—Guidebooks. I. Title.
GV1060.147,S7T68 1993
796.7'S'09783—dc20   92-45659

On the frontispiece: Publisher, balloonist, and motorcyclist Malcolm Forbes discovered Sturgis somewhat late in life, but his visits were memorable ones. Here, in 1989, during the last visit before his death, Forbes and his crew prepared the Harley-Davidson Heritage balloon for a flight over Main Street. Bon voyage, Malcolm, wherever you are.

On the title page: On any day during the Motor Classic, main street will be lined with thousands of motorcycles.

Printed and bound in Hong Kong

Contents

Foreword

Like many motorcycle enthusiasts, I was aware of Sturgis a long time before I ever went there. In the circles in which I moved, the town was always mentioned in the same breath as Hollister, Harleys, outlaws, drunkenness, rape, guns, robbery, and brawls. A scenario sufficient to keep any self-respecting motorcyclist at least 100 miles away. But that was before I began writing about and taking photographs of Harley-Davidson motorcycles and the people who ride them. Thus, it was only a matter of time before I eventually went to Sturgis. I have been back several times since and hope to continue visiting what I consider to be the best motorcycle rally in the world, which also happens to be held in one of my favorite areas of the United States—the Black Hills of South Dakota.

I've been asked by nonmotorcyclist friends why I go to Sturgis. I tell them about the beauty of the Black Hills and the gold rush history of the area, and the great little eateries that charge next to nothing for down-home cooking. That's the easy part. Explaining the flavor of Main Street is something else, and I'm not sure it's entirely possible. Why would anyone, I am asked, want to visit a small town that is filled with the constant thunder of motorcycles, wall-to-wall people, and more tattoo parlors per square mile than anywhere else in the world, and where the shopping fare consists of T-shirts and black leather? The answer, of course, is that these are indeed the things that make it worth visiting. One also finds a strong feeling of belonging here. Sometimes it is hard to explain the essence of a place, but as the T-shirt states, *If You Have to Ask, You Wouldn't Understand.*

If you've ever given any thought to taking a trip to the Black Hills Motorcycle Classic at Sturgis in August but haven't yet made up your mind, my advice is, go and enjoy. Sure there are a lot of Harleys plus guys in leather who look tough. But, there are also a lot of families on Harleys and yuppies on Gold Wings and Beemers. On Main Street there is room for everyone. That is the nature of the place.

Sturgis, however, should be only one stop on your vacation since the Black Hills, in all their summer splendor, are close by and beckon. If you want to explore further afield, the Badlands are to the east and Devils Tower is to the west, just over the state line in Wyoming.

Everyone knows life holds no guarantees, but I'll give you one anyway: Go visit Sturgis and the Black Hills during rally week, and I'll guarantee you'll go back to visit again.

Introduction

It all began back in 1938, when J. C. ("Pappy") Hoel—a Sturgis, South Dakota, resident and Indian motorcycle dealer—suggested that his hometown motorcycle club, the Jackpine Gypsies, organize a two-day rally and race event. Still in the throes of the Great Depression, the Black Hills was a dirt-poor area, but a little over eighty people from Deadwood, Lead (pronounced *Leed*), and Rapid City, all in South Dakota, found enough gas money for the ride to Sturgis. Everyone camped in Pappy and Pearl Hoel's backyard on Junction Avenue, and the first of the two days was devoted to a ride around the scenic Black Hills. On day two, those who were interested removed the lights and fenders from their motorcycle for some racing at the Sturgis Fairgrounds' horse track.

You'll probably never see much in the way of advertising for the Black Hills Motorcycle Classic, as it has come to be known, but if you own a bike, chances are you'll have heard about it. It's one of those word-of-mouth things. That's the way it has always been, and except for three years during World War II, motorcycle enthusiasts in ever-increasing numbers have been converging on Sturgis for what is now a week-long early August event.

Chapter 1

On the Road to Sturgis

The bike has been serviced and stands at the curb. Camping equipment and rolled sleeping bags are secured behind the sissy bar, and the saddlebags are bulging with whatever you or your companion has managed to stuff into them. This year, you've decided to vacation at Sturgis for the Black Hills Motorcycle Classic, and today is the day you leave. It is a 1,000-mile journey, and you are ready! psyched up! can't wait to hit the road!

But how prepared are you for a journey across Middle America in August when the temperature regularly hits 100 degrees Fahrenheit?

Preparation

Before leaving home, sit down with a map and plan your route. While you're figuring out the mileage, also estimate the time you will need to run off those distances—and be conservative. If you like to stay in motels, make appropriate plans. Allow for a schedule that doesn't have you driving all day and most of the night. After all, you will be on vacation, and if you have someone traveling with you, the last thing you need is her or him ragging on you because you haven't allowed time to see any-

thing but the view from the interstate. Either on the way to or on the way home from Sturgis, consider taking in the sights along your route. You'll probably enjoy them and it's amazing how well companions react to "those little touches of thoughtfulness."

Chances are you won't forget your sunglasses, but most guys travelling alone might not normally give a thought to toting along any sunscreen. You wouldn't be caught dead wearing sunscreen, you say. Well, let's discuss that for a moment. Old Mr. Sun, coupled with the wind that blows across those prairies, can make a mess of your face real fast. And after two or three days of riding, you'll be looking right nice for all those pretty young things in Sturgis.

Following the same line of thought, either keep your shoulders and back covered or use sunscreen. Having your skin burned to a crisp and painful to the touch is no way to spend a vacation, especially when part of your time will be spent jostling the crowds on Main Street.

Much of the beauty of the West and Midwest is that which attracted settlers in the first place: wide-open spaces. Even today, there are still hundreds of miles of empty highway and the gas stations tend to be farther apart than you might normally be accustomed to. With this in mind,

Sturgis, here we come!

9

Win a Trophy

Ride to Sturgis—and win a trophy! The rally organizers present awards in eight categories:

1. Oldest rider attending the rally from the United States
2. Oldest rider attending the rally from Canada
3. Female rider coming the longest distance from Canada
4. Male rider coming the longest distance from Canada
5. Female rider coming the longest distance from the United States
6. Male rider coming the longest distance from the United States
7. Female rider coming the longest distance from a foreign country other than Canada
8. Male rider coming the longest distance from a foreign country other than Canada

Entrants in any of the categories must have traveled to Sturgis as the driver or passenger of a motorcycle. Entry blanks are available at rally headquarters on Main Street in Sturgis.

you might want to put a little thought into planning your gas stops, or at the very least topping off more often than you usually would.

Dehydration is something that most of us never give a thought to, but it is worth guarding against on a long motorcycle trip. Prevention is fairly simple: just drink an ample amount of fluids throughout the hottest part of the day. What constitutes fluids? Water is probably the cheapest liquid you can find—unless you're toting along bottles of that $6-a-gallon imported stuff—but fruit juices offer more taste and variety. Beer—as good as it tastes on a hot day—is not a good fluid, for the most obvious of reasons.

One last item: Thunderstorms can develop late in the afternoon, so be prepared for the occasional heavy downpour.

If you need visitor information when you get to South Dakota, try stopping at one of the staffed information centers in the rest areas along the interstate highways. The centers are located at state lines and at various other points along Interstates 90 and 29, the two highways that bisect the state horizontally and vertically.

In South Dakota, helmets are required for riders and passengers under eighteen years of age. Eye protection is also mandated; however, sunglasses or eyeglasses are considered legal protection. In addition, you must have in your possession a valid driver's license—your own would be preferable—and a current registration for the motorcycle you are riding.

Your motorcycle must have mirrors, a working horn, and mufflers that prevent excessive noise. In other words, modified or straight pipes could get you a ticket, as will handlebars that rise 15 inches above your seat.

The speed limit on Interstate 90 is 65mph and is strictly enforced during rally week. Most other highways are posted at 55mph. So slow down, kick back, and enjoy your vacation.

Distance to Sturgis from Major U.S. and Canadian Metropolitan Areas

City	Mileage
Albany, NY	1,788
Albuquerque, NM	824
Atlanta, GA	1,517
Baltimore, MD	1,634

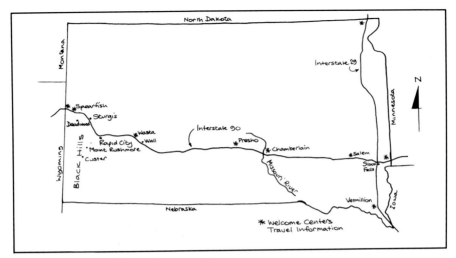

From east or west the easiest route to Sturgis is by Interstate 90.

Billings, MT	317	Milwaukee, WI	841
Birmingham, AL	1,407	Minneapolis, MN	577
Boise, ID	959	Montreal, Que., Can.	1,753
Boston, MA	1,907	Nashville, TN	1,249
Buffalo, NY	1,429	New Orleans, LA	1,504
Calgary, Alta., Can.	936	New York, NY	1,722
Charleston, SC	1,808	Norfolk, VA	1,765
Charleston, WV	1,372	Oklahoma City, OK	855
Cheyenne, WY	314	Omaha, NE	538
Chicago, IL	1,240	Orlando, FL	1,975
Cincinnati, OH	1,226	Philadelphia, PA	1,658
Cleveland, OH	1,240	Phoenix, AZ	1,229
Columbus, OH	1,239	Pittsburgh, PA	1,366
Dallas, TX	1,087	Portland, ME	1,988
Denver, CO	415	Portland, OR	1,266
Des Moines, IA	640	Raleigh, NC	1,697
Detroit, MI	1,195	Regina, Sask., Can.	540
El Paso, TX	1,036	Reno, NV	1,230
Fargo, ND	507	St. Louis, MO	950
Hartford, CT	1,818	Salt Lake City, UT	736
Houston, TX	1,320	San Antonio, TX	1,248
Indianapolis, IN	1,114	San Diego, CA	1,488
Jackson, MS	1,370	San Francisco, CA	1,448
Jacksonville, FL	1,830	Seattle, WA	1,133
Kansas City, KS	695	Toronto, Ont., Can.	1,415
Las Vegas, NV	1,105	Tucson, AZ	1,256
Little Rock, AR	1,136	Vancouver, B.C., Can.	1,277
Los Angeles, CA	1,363	Washington, DC	1,595
Louisville, KY	1,207	Wichita, KS	728
Memphis, TN	1,154	Winnipeg, Man., Can.	678
Miami, FL	2,176		

Chapter 2

Main Street

If you're coming from Rapid City, you'll probably get off Interstate 90 at exit 32. You won't be alone though: a steady stream of bikes will be at each elbow as you ride slowly down Junction Avenue to Main Street.

In the campsite next to the off-ramp, a crowd watches as a young woman bungee jumps from a platform hung below a huge crane. On every empty parcel of land vendors are set up to sell everything from food to Harley parts. The do-it-yourself car wash is doing more business washing bikes than it has all year washing cars, and the local franchised pizza parlor couldn't be busier. The atmosphere is totally carnival.

Towards downtown the traffic gets much thicker, and slowing almost to a stop, you notice license plates from Florida to British Columbia to Maine. Suddenly, after a left turn at a stop sign, you are on Main Street, Sturgis! The street is barricaded to allow only motorcycles to enter, and you run the gauntlet of guys who stand and watch

At rally headquarters, visitors are encouraged to sign in and identify their hometown and country by placing a stickpin in a map. By late afternoon, every parking spot on Main Street is taken and the sidewalks are so jammed that the crowds overflow into the street.

those who enter and leave. Mostly they just like to see the bikes, but there are those who encourage women to lift their tank tops and smile for the camera.

No one has to give a reason for riding down Main Street. You do it because you've ridden 1,000 miles to get here and it's the thing to do. It's strutting your stuff adult style. And, once in a great while, there's no better ego trip.

When the bikes stop to let someone reverse into an empty parking spot, you have time to look around. The street is a solid mass of people, many of whom slowly thread their way along the sidewalks past others who stand watching the continuous parade of bikes and riders. The sound of V-twins accelerating and decelerating reverberates off the buildings, but after a time, you don't hear them. Signs of every size and description assault the senses. They advertise concerts, races, rodeos, campsites, restaurants, bars, pinstriping, oil changes. And they take up every available space on walls, utility poles, and storefront windows. As on Junction Avenue, vendors are every place you look. They set up shop in alleys, basements, empty corner lots, and stores that have been emptied of their more normal merchandise for the duration of the rally. Everywhere

Main Street is a great place for meeting people you haven't seen in a while.

there is food for sale: Gyros across the street, buffalo burgers down the street, Indian tacos here, and that old standby the Polish (pass the antacids) sausage sandwich over there. Tattoos are also big business, and every once in a while, a guy or gal walks by with a fresh bandage taped to a part of his or her body.

The mix of people is incredibly varied. Families from Iowa traveling the Black Hills share the crowded sidewalks with bikers they would probably make a point to cross the street to get away from back home. But this is the Black Hills Motorcycle Classic, and things are a little bit different around here during rally week.

Welcome to Sturgis.

The Sturgis Police Department, temporarily enlarged for the rally, keeps a constant vigil on Main Street. To the officers' credit, they try to stay low-key.

Strutting your stuff is what Main Street is all about.

Riding up one side of Main Street and down the other goes on well into the early hours of the next morning.

A Vincent—a British V-twin of fifties vintage—adds an international flavor to Main Street.

Just watch where you stand when this bike comes by.

Chapter 3

Where to Camp, Sleep, and Eat

One neat thing about Sturgis is that if you plan on camping, you can choose from numerous campsites. Chances are, you won't need to make any reservations at most of the private campsites, since no matter how full they might initially appear, they always seem to find room for one more tent. Should you feel more comfortable with a reservation, however, phone numbers are included with the campground listings at the end of this chapter. If, on the other hand, you are more comfortable in a motel or hotel, you may have some difficulty if you don't have a reservation. But more on that later.

Camping in Sturgis tends to be drawn along two very deliberate lines: party-hearty style and family style. The only explanation needed for a party-hearty campground is that you may have trouble getting any sleep, as the music and the partying tend to go on all night. Families with small children might be advised to look elsewhere. But how does one gauge the partying index of a particular campground? The simplest and most reliable way we know is to ask

Numerous campsites are available in Sturgis and the Black Hills. Pick one that matches your lifestyle; at some facilities, you may not get much in the way of sleep.

some of the other campers before you check in.

A number of temporary campgrounds in the area open for just a couple of weeks around rally time. Overall, some might be better than others, but they all offer such basics as clean showers and toilets, plus laundry facilities. Some even offer food, a resident tattoo artist, swap meet merchandise, and nightly entertainment in the form of live bands. If you ride into Sturgis without a clue as to where the various campgrounds are—having left your copy of this book at home—it will not take long to locate them. Stop off at rally headquarters in the armory on Main Street, and you will find flyers for practically every campground within 50 miles and instructions on how to get there. You will also find banners giving directions on walls, and flyers tacked to every utility pole in town, so you shouldn't have any trouble locating somewhere to pitch the old tent.

If you are less inclined to a social atmosphere or enjoy a place where the view is important, you might enjoy camping on national forest land in the Black Hills. The Forest Service does impose some restrictions on length of stay and open fires, and at some campsites, toilet facilities are practically nonexistent. Many would argue, however, that camping in a meadow beside a mountain stream is well worth the inconvenience. Reservations are required for a number of the Black Hills National Forest campsites, and information can be found at the end of this chapter.

You may prefer a motel or hotel to camping. Motels can be found in Sturgis and numerous lodging places are located throughout the Black Hills area, but during rally week, they are filled to capacity. In fact, many returning visitors make their reservations up to a year in advance. The farther from Sturgis you are prepared to stay, the greater the room availability. An inventory of warm and dry shelters follows the campground list at the end of this chapter.

Where to eat is never a problem at Sturgis, since dozens of vendors sell everything from sausage to tacos to burgers. The problem with this type of diet is that your stomach soon begins to crave more regular food. Sturgis does have a limited number of restaurants, and the Black Hills area has numerous others that serve home-style cooking, and some that offer all-you-can-eat buffets, which are very popular during rally week.

If you are on a budget, some good eating bargains can be found around Sturgis. Churches, the senior citizen center, a local Alcoholics Anonymous chapter, and the Veterans Club serve all-you-can-eat pancake breakfasts for what seems to be less money than the food itself costs.

Not unexpectedly, Sturgis has a few laws you are supposed to comply with. Driving while intoxicated will get you a night in the slammer and the minimum of a healthy fine. The city officials also don't like people drinking alcohol in a public place, or whizzing in alleys when they can't find a john. The best advice is to be straight while within city limits, and

Some uncrowded campsites can be found quite close to Sturgis. You might want to stay only one night at a time until you find one you like. Many campsites serve food and beer, and plow profits back into permanent structures.

party in the campsites where you won't be hassled.

For the record, I haven't tried many of the campgrounds, motels, and restaurants listed here, and I make no claims for any of them—although I do have my favorites, and they are included. You will find that in general, the Black Hills offers value for your money and, unlike large metropolitan areas, people who are genuinely interested in making sure you have a good time.

Campgrounds

Since most visitors spend time at the Black Hills Classic, the following list of campgrounds begins with those closest to Sturgis, and radiates outwards to Devils Tower to the west, Hot Springs to the south, and the Badlands to the east.

Sturgis Camping

Bear Butte Creek Campground
East of Sturgis on State Hwy. 34
(605)347-5715
Sturgis, SD. 57785

Bear Butte State Park
5 miles east of Sturgis on State Hwy. 79
Limited number of shaded sites, no shower or recreational vehicle (RV) hookups
(605)347-5240
Box 688, Sturgis, SD. 57785

Boulder Park Campground
I-90, exit 30, 5½ miles west of Sturgis on State U.S. Hwy. 14A
Shade trees, hot showers, RV hookups, tables, quiet and cool setting
(605)347-3222
Box 806, Boulder Canyon, Sturgis, SD. 57785

Buffalo Chip Campground
East of Sturgis on State Hwy. 34, at Airport Rd.
(605)892-2033

1113 5th Ave., Belle Fourche, SD. 57717

Days End Campground
I-90, exit 30
65 tent sites, RV hookups, showers, laundry, groceries, RV supplies
(605)347-2331
HC 55, Box 136, Sturgis, SD. 57785

Eagle's Landing Campground
I-90, exit 30, ½ mile west of Sturgis on North Service Rd.
(308)762-2735
Sturgis, SD. 57785

Glencoe Camp Resort
2 miles east of Sturgis on State Hwy. 34
Shaded camping, showers, 24-hour concessions, free firewood, free morning coffee, RVs for rent
(605)347-4712
PO Box 592, Sturgis, SD. 57785

Hog Campground
5 miles north of drag strip on State Hwy. 79
Showers, shade, quiet
(605)347-2431
Sturgis, SD. 57785

Hog Heaven
I-90, exit 30.
320 secluded acres with lots of shade, hot showers, food, live bands, bar, concessions
(605)348-5175
Box 2977, Rapid City, SD. 57709

Lund's Campground
I-90, exit 30, ½ mile past Super 8 Motel on Whitewood Rd.
(605)347-4833
Box 308, Sturgis, SD. 57785

Rushmore Shadows Resort
40 minutes south of Sturgis on U.S. Hwy. 16
200 campsites, clubhouse, pool, showers, laundry, store, breakfast

and lunch daily
(605)343-4544
PO Box 1696, Rapid City, SD 57709

Sturgis Motorcycle Campground
2 blocks off I-90, exit 32
Shade trees, showers, concession
stand, free firewood
(816)566-3366
13422 S. Noel Road, Lee Summit,
MO. 64063

Sturgis Run Cycle Camp
2160 Dolan Creek Rd.
1 mile from downtown Sturgis and ¼
mile from fairgrounds
80 acres, hot showers, food
(605)347-4395
Sturgis, SD. 57785

Vanocker Campground
I-90, exit 32
(605)347-4556
PO Box 1075, Sturgis, SD. 57785

Piedmont Valley Camping
Elk Creek Campground and Lodge
I-90, exit 46
Facilities accessible to handicapped
visitors, shaded sites, RV hookups,
laundry, showers, pool
(605)787-4884
HCR 80, Box 767, Piedmont, SD.
57769

Mooney's Hog Farm and
Campground
I-90, exit 46, Elk Creek Rd.
Shaded camping, showers, RVs
welcome
(605)787-4355
Box 2630, Black Hawk, SD. 57718

Tilford Estates Campground
I-90, exit 40
Some shaded campsites, showers,
food
(605)347-3848
Piedmont, SD. 57769

Tilford Gulch Campground
From Rapid City: I-90, exit 44, 3½

miles north
From Sturgis: I-90, exit 40, 1½ miles
south
Some shade, showers, meals, group
rates
(800)827-1573
HCR 80, Box 861-10, Piedmont, SD.
57769

Deadwood Camping
Custer Crossing Campground
15 miles south of Deadwood on U.S.
Hwy. 385
RV hookups, convenience store,
groceries
(605)584-1009
HCR 73, Box 1527, Deadwood, SD.
57732

Deadwood KOA
1 mile west of Deadwood on U.S.
Hwy. 14A
RV hookups, pool, store, laundry,
playground
(605)578-3830
PO Box 451VG, Deadwood, SD.
57732

Fish 'N Fry Campground
5 miles south of Deadwood on U.S.
Hwy. 385
Full RV hookups, dump station,
showers, heated pool, restaurant,
groceries
(605)578-2150
Nemo Rt., Box 801, Deadwood, SD.
57732

Hidden Valley Campground
South of Deadwood on U.S. Hwy.
385
Campsites in pines, RV hookups,
showers, laundry, store, fire grates
and tables at each site, dump
station
(605)578-1342
HC 73, Box 1115, Deadwood, SD.
57732

Wild Bill's Campground
5 miles south of Lead-Deadwood on
U.S. Hwy. 385

Shaded and creekside sites, cabins
with kitchenettes, full RV
hookups, dump station, showers,
laundry, pool, playground,
restaurant
(605)578-2800
HC 73, Box 1101, Deadwood, SD.
57732

Belle Fourche Camping

Riverside Campground
Full hookups, showers, laundry,
firewood, playground
(605)892-6446
PO Box 121, Belle Fourche, SD.
57717

Spearfish Camping

Centennial Campground
3 miles East of Spearfish on U.S.
Hwy. 85
Full hookups, showers
(605)642-7941
Spearfish, SD. 57783

Chris's Campground
I-90, exit 14, $^1/_2$ mile south on

Christensen Dr.
Facilities accessible to handicapped
visitors, shaded sites, showers,
laundry, heated pool, rec room
(605)642-2239
Spearfish, SD. 57783

City Campground
I-90 exit 12
Facilities accessible to handicapped
visitors, shaded sites, full hookups,
showers, pool
(605)642-3744
722 Main St.
Spearfish, SD. 57783

KOA Spearfish
I-90, exit 10, $^1/_4$ mile west on service
road
Kamp Kabins, RV hookups, heated
pool, playground
(605)642-4633
Box 429, Spearfish, SD. 57783

Mountain View Campground
I-90, exit 14, $^1/_2$ mile south on
Christensen Dr.

*Live bands are a big part of Sturgis, and in
some campgrounds, the music does not
stop until the wee hours.*

Facilities accessible to handicapped
visitors, shaded and level sites, RV
hookups, showers, heated pool,
groceries, playground, game room
(605)642-2170
Rt. 2, Box 442, Spearfish, SD. 57783

Hill City Camping

Crooked Creek RV Park,
Campground and Cabins
2 miles north of junction of State
Hwy. 244 and U.S. Hwy. 385
Level and grassy sites, cabins, RV
hookups, dump station, showers,
laundry, pool, playground, tables
(605)574-2418
Box 603, Hill City, SD. 57745

Forks Campground
4 miles north of Hill City at junction
of U.S. Hwys. 16 and 385
Facilities accessible to handicapped
visitors, groceries, RV hookups,
laundry, dump station, playground
(605)574-2702
HCR 87, Box 70, Hill City, SD. 57745

Horse Thief Resort Campground
3 miles south of Hill City on U.S.
Hwy. 385, then 2 miles south on
State Hwy. 87
Shaded sites, full RV hookups,
heated pool, laundry, store,
firewood
(605)574-2668
PO Box 307, Hill City, SD. 57745

Lazy S Campground
15 miles northwest of Hill City on
County Rd. 307
Secluded RV hookups, showers,
dump station, fire grates
(605)574-2649
HCR 87, Box 42, Hill City, SD. 57745

Mount Rushmore KOA
5 miles west of Mt. Rushmore on
State Hwy. 244
Cabins, heated pool, hot tub, free
movies, restaurant
(605)574-2525
Box 295V, Hill City, SD. 57745

Rafter J Bar Ranch Campground
Junction of U.S. Hwy. 16/385 and
State Hwy. 87
Shaded sites, RV hookups, heated
pool, laundry, groceries, firewood,
rec room, playground
(605)574-2527
Box 128, Hill City, SD. 57745

Keystone Camping

Battle Creek Campground
3/4 mile west of Keystone on County
Rd.323
Facilities accessible to handicapped
visitors, secluded and quiet
setting, full RV hookups, dump
station, tepee camping, showers,
ministore
(605)666-4557
Keystone, SD. 57751

Elk Haven
U.S. Hwy. 16A, at northern edge of
Custer State Park
Full RV hookups, cabins, campsites,
showers, laundry, grocery store,
dump station
(605)666-4856
Box 17, Keystone, SD. 57751

Kemp's Kamp
1 1/2 miles west of Keystone on
County Rd. 323
Full RV hookups, laundry, showers,
cabins, pool, picnic tables
(605)666-4654
Keystone, SD. 57751

Miner's RV Park
U.S. Hwy. 16A
Facilities accessible to handicapped
visitors, shaded sites, RV hookups,
tent sites, store, laundry, heated
pool and hot tub, restaurant
(605)666-4456 or (800)843-1300
Box 157, Keystone, SD. 57751

Rushmore Resort Campground and
Motel
7 miles south of Mt. Rushmore on
U.S. Hwy. 16A
Facilities accessible to handicapped

visitors, 80 secluded acres, RV
hooking, pool, groceries, motel
rooms, hiking, horses, fishing lake
(605)666-4605
Box 124, Keystone, SD. 57751

Rapid City Camping

Berry Patch Campground
I-90, exit 60
Level sites, full RV hookups,
showers, heated pool, laundry,
groceries, game room, playground
(800)658-4566
1860 E. North St., Rapid City, SD.
57701

Four B's Campground
3 1/2 miles south of Rapid City on U.S.
Hwy. 16
116 level sites, some shaded; full RV
hookups; showers; heated pool;
laundry; groceries; game room;
playground; security lights
(605)341-8554
Rapid City, SD. 57701

Happy Holiday Campground and
Motel
5 1/2 miles south of Rapid City on U.S.
Hwy. 16
208 full RV hookups, laundry,
showers, heated pool, rec room,
playground, groceries, firewood
(605)342-7365
HC 33, Box 8905, Rapid City, SD.
57701

Lake Park Campground
I-90, exit 57, south to State Hwy.
44W, 4 1/2 miles west to Chapel Ln.,
left to campground
Shaded sites, full RV hookups,
showers, laundry, store, heated
pool
(605)341-5320 or (605)348-2627
2850 Chapel Lane, Rapid City, SD.
57702

Lazy J RV Park and Campground
1 mile south of Rapid City on U.S.
Hwy. 16

Full RV hookups, individual tent
sites, showers, pool, laundry,
groceries, playground, rec room
(605)342-2751
4110 S. U.S. Hwy. 16, Rapid City, SD.
57701

Mount Rushmore KOA
5 miles west of Mt. Rushmore on
State Hwy. 244
Shaded sites, full RV hookups, Kamp
Kabins, showers, laundry,
groceries, restaurant, firewood,
picnic tables
(605)574-2525, (800)233-4331
Box 295, Hill City, SD. 57745

Rapid City KOA
I-90, exit 61, 2 1/2 miles south
Facilities accessible to handicapped
visitors, Kamp Kabins, pool and
spa, free breakfast daily
(605)348-2111, (800)852-2946
PO Box 2592, Rapid City, SD. 57709

Red Arrow Camping Ranch
I-90, exits 48 and 51
Shaded sites, full RV hookups, pool
(605)787-4841
Rt 1, Box 228, Black Hawk, SD.
57718

Trout Haven Campground
19 miles west of Rapid City on U.S.
Hwy. 385
Cool climate in Black Hills, full RV
hookups, store and cafe, well-
stocked small trout lake
(605)342-6009
Nemo Rt., Deadwood, SD. 57732

Wooded Acres Campground
9 miles southwest of Rapid City on
U.S. Hwy. 16
Shaded sites, full RV hookups,
showers, laundry, groceries, pool,
picnic tables, firewood
(605)342-5368
Keystone Rt., Box 1113, Rapid City,
SD. 57701

Black Hills National Forest Camping

For more information on camping in the Black Hills, write or call the national forest:
Black Hills National Forest
RR 2, Box 200
Custer, SD 57730
(605)673-2251

Bear Gulch Campground
On Pactola Reservoir, 24 miles west of Rapid City; U.S. Hwy. 385 to Black Forest Inn intersection, then Forest Service Rds. (FSRs) 258, 251, and 253
4,600-foot altitude; 8 shoreline sites for tents, travel trailers, and RVs; reservation needed; 10-day limit; fee charged

Bearlodge Campground
25 miles west of Belle Fourche on Wyoming Hwy. 24
7 sites for tents, travel trailers, and RVs; no fee

Beaver Creek Campground
19 miles north of Newcastle, Wyoming, on U.S. Hwy. 85 to Four Corners, then 6 miles east on FSRs 810, 811, and 111
8 streamside sites for tents, travel trailers, and RVs; 10-day limit; no fee charged

Bismark Lake Campground
4 miles east of Custer on U.S. Hwy. 16A
28 lakeside sites for tents, travel trailers, and RVs; 10-day limit; fee charged

Black Fox Campground
7 miles west of Rochford on FSR 231
9 streamside sites for tents, travel trailers, and RVs; 10-day limit; no fee charged

Boxelder Forks Campground
2 miles west of Nemo on FSR 140
15 sites for tents, travel trailers, and RVs; 10-day limit; fee charged

Castle Peak Campground
20 miles northwest of Hill City on County Road 17, then FSRs 231 and 181
Undeveloped road to 9 streamside sites for tents; 10-day limit; no fee charged

Commanche Park Campground
7 miles west of Custer on U.S. Hwy. 16
34 sites for tents, travel trailers, and RVs; 10-day limit; fee charged

Cook Lake Campground
20 miles north of Sundance, Wyoming; follow FSRs 843 and 842
30 lakeside sites for tents, travel trailers, and RVs; 10-day limit; fee charged

Custer Trail Campground
23 miles northwest of Hill City; follow County Road 17 to north side of Deerfield Lake, then FSR 417 to lakeside
Boat ramp with parking for 16 travel trailers or RVs; 3-day limit; no fee charged

Dalton Lake Campground
7 miles northeast of Nemo; follow FSRs 135 and 224
11 sites for tents, travel trailers, and RVs; 10-day limit; fee charged

Ditch Creek Campground
4 miles south of Deerfield Lake on FSR 291
13 sites for tents, travel trailers, and RVs; 10-day limit; fee charged

Dutchman Campground
2 miles north on FSR 607, off County Road 17 at Deerfield Lake
45 lakeside sites for tents, travel

trailers, and RVs; 10-day limit; fee charged

Hanna Campground
9 miles southwest of Lead on U.S. Hwy. 85, then 2 miles south on FSR 196
13 streamside sites for tents, travel trailers, and RVs; 10-day limit; fee charged

Horsethief Lake Campground
1 mile north of Mt. Rushmore on State Hwy. 244
36 lakeside sites for tents, travel trailers, and RVs; 3-day limit; fee charged

Moon Campground
9 miles east of Newcastle, Wyoming, on U.S. Hwy. 16, then 16 miles north on FSR 117
3 sites for tents, travel trailers, and RVs; 10-day limit; no fee charged

Oreville Campground
4 miles south of Hill City on U.S. Hwy. 16/385
26 sites for tents, travel trailers, and RVs; 10-day limit; fee charged

Pactola Campground
West of Rapid City on south shore of Pactola Reservoir
80 lakeside sites for tents, travel trailers, and RVs; 10-day limit; fee charged

Red Bank Spring Campground
9 miles east of Newcastle, Wyoming, on U.S. Hwy. 16, then 20 miles north on SFSR 117, then 1 mile east on FSR 294
5 pondside sites for tents, travel trailers, and RVs; 10-day limit; no fee charged

Reuter Campground
2 miles west of Sundance, Wyoming, on U.S. Hwy. 14, then 3 miles north on FSR 843

24 sites for tents, travel trailers, and RVs; 10-day limit; fee charged

Rifle Pit Campground
16 miles south of Custer on U.S. Hwy. 385
26 sites for tents, travel trailers, and RVs; 10-day limit; fee charged

Rod and Gun Campground
13 miles south of Spearfish on U.S. Hwy. 14A to Savoy, then 2 miles west on FSR 222
7 streamside sites for tents, travel trailers, and RVs; 10-day limit; fee charged

Roubaix Lake Campground
13 miles south of Deadwood on U.S. Hwy. 385, then west on FSR 255
56 lakeside sites for tents, travel trailers, and RVs; 10-day limit; fee charged

Sheridan Lake North Cove Campground
15 miles southwest of Rapid City on north shore of Sheridan Lake
58 lakeside sites within 5 group areas for tents, travel trailers, and RVs; reservation needed; 10-day limit; group rate charged

Sheridan Lake Southside Campground
17 miles southwest of Rapid City on south shore of Sheridan Lake
128 lakeside sites for tents, travel trailers, and RVs; 10-day limit; fee charged

Timon Campground
15 miles south of Spearfish on U.S. Hwy. 14A to Savoy, then west on FSR 222
7 streamside sites for tents, travel trailers, and RVs; 10-day limit; fee charged

Whitetail Campground
15 miles northwest of Hill City;

County Road 17 to Deerfield Lake, then 1 mile on FSR 421
17 lakeside sites for tents, travel trailers, and RVs; 10-day limit; fee charged

Willow Creek Horse Camp
3 miles south of Hill City on U.S. Hwy. 16/385, then east on State Hwy. 244
12 streamside sites for tents, travel trailers, RVs, and horse trailers; reservation needed; 10-day limit; group rate charged

Custer State Park Camping

Entrance licenses are now required year-round in South Dakota state parks. Camping fees are collected year-round as well. For more information, write or call the park:
Custer State Park
Box 70
Custer, SD 57730
(605)255-4464

Blue Bell Campground
In Custer State Park, near French Creek
35 sites, rest rooms, showers, playground equipment, no RV hookups

Center Lake Campground
In Custer State Park, near Black Hills Playhouse
75 sites, pit toilets, showers, playground equipment, no RV hookups

Game Lodge Campground
In Custer State Park, near State Game Lodge
55 cool and shady creekside sites, rest rooms, showers, playground equipment, no RV hookups, dump station

Grace Coolidge Campground
In Custer State Park, adjacent to Grace Coolidge Creek and walk-

in fishing area
23 sites, rest rooms, showers, no RV hookups

Legion Lake Campground
In central part of Custer State Park
25 sites, rest rooms, showers, playground equipment, no RV hookups

Stockade Lake Campground
In Custer State Park
85 sites, pit toilets, showers, no RV hookups

Sylvan Lake Campground
In Custer State Park, adjacent to Needles Hwy.
40 sites, rest rooms, showers, Sylvan Lake Resort and store close-by, no RV hookups

Wind Cave National Park Camping
Wind Cave Campground
12 miles north of Hot Springs on U.S. Hwy. 385

Custer Camping
American President's Campground
1 mile east of Custer on U.S. Hwy. 16A
20 sites, full RV hookups, heated pool and spa, showers, laundry, store
(605)673-3373
PO Box 446, Custer, SD. 57730

Big Pine Campground
2 miles west of Custer on U.S. Hwy. 16
85 shaded and level sites, full RV hookups, showers, laundry, store, game room, fireplaces, firewood
(605)673-4054
Rt. 1, Box 52, Custer, SD. 57730

Custer/Crazy Horse KOA
1 mile north of Custer on U.S. Hwy 16/385
Campsites in pines, Kamp Kabins,

heated pool, laundry, arcade,
playground
(800)658-5455
Rt. 2, Box 3030, Custer, SD. 57730

Flintstones Bedrock City
U.S. Hwy. 16 in Custer
Facilities accessible to handicapped
visitors, heated pool, laundry,
playground
(605)673-4079
Box 649, Custer, SD. 57730

Hot Springs Camping
Hot Springs KOA
1/2 mile north of U.S. Hwy. 385 on
State Hwy. 79
Full RV hookups, Kamp Kabins, pool,
store
(605)745-6996
Hot Springs, SD. 57747

Larive Lake Resort and Campground
1/2 mile north of Hot Springs on U.S.
Hwy. 385
Shaded and level sites, full RV
hookups, showers, laundry, picnic
tables, swimming
(605)745-3993
PO Box 33, Hot Springs, SD. 57747

Wasta Camping
Bruce's Campground
I-90, exit 99
Shaded sites, full RV hookups,
showers, laundry
(605) 993-3135
Box 13, Wasta, SD. 57791

Wall Camping
Arrow Campground
I-90, exit 109 or 110
Full RV hookups, showers, laundry,
store, pool
(605)279-2112
Box 366, Wall, SD. 57790

Sleepy Hollow Campground
I-90, exit 109 or 110 to 4th Ave.
Facilities accessible to handicapped
visitors, full RV hookups, dump
station, laundry, picnic tables,

groceries, playground, pool
(605)279-2100
Box 101, Wall, SD. 57790

Badlands National Park Camping
Badlands Interior Campground and
Motel
I-90, exit 131; Hwy 44, 2 miles from
Interior
Facilities accessible to handicapped
visitors, full RV hookups, camping
cabins, laundry, pool, groceries,
playground
(605)433-5335 or (800)999-6116
HC 54, Box 115, Interior, SD. 57750

Badlands KOA Campground
I-90, exit 131; State Hwy. 377 south
to Interior, then 4 miles east on
State Hwy. 44.
Kamp Kabins, pool
(800)628-0064
HC 54, Box 1, Interior, SD. 57750

Cedar Pass Campground
State Hwy. 240 at Cedar Pass
Interior, SD. 57750

Circle 10 Campground
I-90, exit 131
Shaded tent and RV sites, camping
cabins, showers, laundry, pool,
playground, cafe
(605)386-2601
Rt. 1, Box 51 1/2, Philip, SD. 57567

Kadoka Camping
Dirk's Campground
I-90, exit 150
Facilities accessible to handicapped
visitors, full RV hookups, laundry,
groceries, playground
(605)673-3370
Rt. 2, Box 199, Kadoka, SD. 57543

Kadoka Campground
I-90, exit 150
Facilities accessible to handicapped
visitors, shady and grassy sites, full
RV hookups, Laundromat, heated
pool, playground

(605)837-2243
Box 399, Kadoka, SD. 57543

Ponderosa RV Park
I-90, exit 150 to business loop
Shaded and level sites, full RV
 hookups, showers, laundry, heated
 pool, groceries
(605)837-2362
PO Box 64, Kadoka, SD. 57543

Devils Tower, Wyoming, Camping

Devils Tower KOA
State Hwy. 110, at entrance to tower
Facilities accessible to handicapped
 visitors, full RV hookups, laundry,
 heated pool, groceries, full-service
 restaurant
(307)467-5395
Box 77, Devils Tower, WY. 82714

Motels, Hotels, Resorts, Lodges, Inns, and Bed and Breakfasts

The following is a fairly comprehensive list, but it is by no means complete. Where information is available, it is included. Certain things, however, have been omitted. For example, the availability of television is not included because it is probably difficult to find a motel or hotel in the United States that does not have a color television set and cable service in every room. The availability of free ice is also missing, as this item is not considered a luxury. In addition, accepted credit cards are not given, since any of the major cards should be welcomed for payment.

On the other hand, if a lodging is air conditioned—another basic for most of us—notation has been made to that effect. It is important to note that the majority of hotels and motels—especially national-chain motels—are air conditioned, even if not stated. Nights in the Black Hills are generally cool and comfortable, but heat waves are not uncommon, with the result that sleeping can be uncomfortable without air conditioning.

Again, since most visitors spend time at the Black Hills Classic, the following list begins with those closest to Sturgis, and radiates outwards.

Sturgis Lodging

Best Western Philtown Inn
I-90, exit 32, Junction Ave.
(605)347-3604 or (800)528-1234
PO Box 777, Sturgis, SD. 57785

Junction Inn
1802 Junction Ave.
I-90, exit 32
(605)347-5675 or (800)658-3695
Sturgis, SD. 57785

Lantern Motel
1706 Junction Ave.
Some kitchens, air conditioning,
 playground
(605)347-4511
Sturgis, SD. 57785

Starlite Motel
2426 Junction Ave.
(605)347-2506 or (800)658-3695
Sturgis, SD. 57785

Super 8 Motel
I-90, exit 30
(605)347-4447 or (800)800-8000
PO Box 703, Sturgis, SD. 57785

Piedmont Valley Lodging

Covered Wagon Motel
I-90, exits 46 and 48
(605)787-4440
Piedmont, SD. 57769

Deadwood Lodging

The Adams House Bed and Breakfast
22 Van Buren
1892 Victorian home furnished with
 antiques, no smoking or pets, no
 children under 12
(605)578-3877
Deadwood, SD. 57732

All Season's Budget Motel
410 Cliff St.
At junction of U.S. Hwys. 385 and
85
Singles, doubles, divided doubles,
kitchenettes, air conditioning, at-
door parking, restaurants nearby
(605)578-2529
Deadwood, SD. 57732

All Season's Motel and Casino
801 Upper Main St.
Facilities accessible to handicapped
visitors, air conditioning,
Laundromat, restaurant
(605)578-2393
Deadwood, SD. 57732

Barefoot Condominiums
At Terry Peak
2- or 3-bedroom condos, full
kitchens, sauna, daily rates
available
(605)584-1577
HC 37, Box 924, Lead, SD. 57754

Best Western Hickok House
137 Charles St.
(605)578-1611 or (800)528-1234
Deadwood, SD. 57732

Days Inn
68 Main St.
U.S. Hwys. 14A and 85
(800)526-8277
Deadwood, SD. 57732

Deadwood Gulch Resort
South of Main St. on U.S. Hwy. 85
Spa, restaurant, lounge,
convenience store
(605)578-1294 or (800)695-1876
Deadwood, SD. 57732

El Rancho Motel
U.S. Hwy. 85
Refrigerators, air conditioning,
playground, restaurants close-by
(605)578-2725
Deadwood, SD. 57732

First Gold Hotel
270 Main St.
24-hour full-service restaurant
(605)578-2529 or (800)274-1876
Deadwood, SD. 57732

4 U Motel
296 Main St.
AAA (Automobile Association of
America) rated, children under 6
free, group rates, restaurant next-
door
(605)578-3464
Deadwood, SD. 57732

Franklin Hotel and Motor Inn
700 Main St.
Historic 1903 hotel, dining room,
Irish pub, children under 12 free
(605)578-2241, (800)688-1876
(South Dakota only), or
(800)421-6662
Deadwood, SD. 57732

Gold Diggers Hotel
629 Main St.
(605)578-3213 or (800)456-2023
Deadwood, SD. 57732

Lariat Motel
360 Main St.
Group rates, family units
(605)578-1500
Deadwood, SD. 57732

Mountain Creek Lodge
7 miles south of Deadwood on U.S.
Hwy. 385
Motel, cabins, cafe, playground
(605)578-3449
HC 73, Box 1116, Deadwood, SD.
57732

76 Motel
Intersection of U.S. Hwys. 14A and
85
AAA, air conditioning, full-service
restaurant, group rates,
nonsmoking rooms
(605)578-3476
Deadwood, SD. 57732

Super 8 Motel
U.S. Hwy. 385S
(605)578-2535 or (800)800-8000
Deadwood, SD. 57732

Lead Lodging

Best Western Golden Hills Resort
900 Miner's Ave.
Facilities accessible to handicapped
  visitors, air conditioning,
  restaurant, pool, lounge,
  entertainment
(800)528-1234
Lead, SD. 57754

Cheyenne Crossing Bed and
  Breakfast
Junction of U.S. Hwys. 14A and 85
(605)584-3510
Lead, SD. 57754

Ponderosa Motor Lodge
U.S. Hwy. 14A
(605)584-3321
Lead, SD. 57754

Terry Peak Lodge
1- or 2-bedroom condos, full
  kitchens, heated pool, sauna
(605)584-2723
HC 37, Box 917, Lead, SD. 57754

Whitetale Court Motel
1 mile south of Lead on U.S. Hwy. 85
Cabins, kitchenettes, motel rooms
(605)584-3315
PO Box 596, Lead, SD. 57754

Hill City Lodging

Best Western Golden Spike Inn
U.S. Hwys. 16/385
Facilities accessible to handicapped
  visitors, heated pool, hot tub
(605)574-2577 or (800)528-1234
PO Box 300, Hill City, SD. 57745

Black Hills Llama Lodge
5½ miles west of Hill City
Antique furnishings, shared bath,
  kitchen, laundry
(605)574-2455
PO Box 109, Hill City, SD. 57745

Blue Spruce Valley Cabins and
  Campground
4 miles south of Hill City on U.S.
  Hwy. 16/385
Cabins, groceries, shady campsites
(605)574-2366
PO Box 468, Hill City, SD. 57745

Cozy Motel
417 Main St.
Some kitchens, air conditioning, at-
  door parking, Laundromat, special
  3-day rates
(605)574-2411
Box 172, Hill City, SD. 57745

Harney Camp Cabins
4 miles south of Hill City on Needles
  Hwy., at Sylvan Lake
Facilities accessible to handicapped
  visitors, various sizes of cabins
  with kitchen, hot tub
(605)574-2594
Box 615, Hill City, SD. 57745

Harney Peak Motel
U.S. Hwy. 16/385 in downtown Hill
  City
Some kitchenettes, at-door parking,
  cafes and stores within walking
  distance
(605)574-2544
Box 383, Hill City, SD. 57745

The Homestead
10 miles from Mt. Rushmore
5,000-square-foot home on 50
  acres, sleeping for 2–24
(605)574-4226
Box 635, Hill City, SD. 57745

Jay's Motel and Cottages
¾ mile south of downtown Hill City
  on U.S. Hwy. 16/385
Large cottages, full kitchens,
  playground, special 3-day rates
(605)574-2364
Box 63, Hill City, SD. 57745

Lantern Inn Motel
AAA; single, double, and adjoining

rooms; air conditioning;
restaurant close-by; playground;
picnic tables
(605)574-2582 or (800)843-1300
PO Box 744, Hill City, SD. 57745

Lewis Park Cabins and Motel
2 blocks west of Main St.
Motel units and cabins with kitchens
(605)574-2565
PO Box 332, Hill City, SD. 57745

Lode Stone Motel
1 1/2 miles east of Hill City
Facilities accessible to handicapped
visitors, log cabins with private
bathrooms, kitchens
(605)574-2347
HCR 87, Box 57, Hill City, SD. 57745

Palmer Gulch Lodge
5 miles west of Mt. Rushmore on
State Hwy. 244
1- to 3-bedroom cabins, some with
kitchens; air conditioning; heated
pool; campground; restaurant
(605)574-2525
Box 295, Hill City, SD. 57745

Pine Rest Cabins
1 mile south of Hill City
Cabins with kitchens, playground
(605)574-2416
PO Box 377, Hill City, SD. 57745

Pines Edge Motel
4 miles northeast of Hill City, at
junction of U.S. Hwys. 16 and 385
Facilities accessible to handicapped
visitors, family-size rooms, air
conditioning
(605)574-2236
Keystone Rt., Box 2406, Rapid City,
SD. 57702

Robins Roost Cabins
2 miles east of Hill City off U.S. Hwy.
16/385
Cabins with kitchens, family focus,
10pm–7am quiet time
(605)574-2252
HCR 87, Box 62, Hill City, SD. 57745

Spring Creek Inn
1 mile east of Hill City
Motel units, cottages, kitchenettes,
air conditioning, playground
(605)574-2591
Hill City, SD. 57745

Super 8 Motel
U.S Hwy. 16/385 at Deerfield Rd.
and Main St.
(605)574-4141 or (800)800-8000
PO Box 555, Hill City, SD. 57745

Keystone Lodging

Battle Creek Motor Inn
1 mile east of traffic signal on State
Hwy. 40
Facilities accessible to handicapped
visitors, air conditioning, pool
(605)666-4417
HC 33, Box 108, Keystone, SD.
57751

Bed and Breakfast Inn
3 blocks east of traffic signal on State
Hwy. 40
Private entrance, private bath, air
conditioning, family units,
continental breakfast
(605)666-4490
Box 154, Keystone, SD. 57751

Best Western Four President's Motel
U.S. Hwy. 16A
Facilities accessible to handicapped
visitors, air conditioning,
restaurants nearby
(605)666-4472 or (800)528-1234
Box 690, Keystone, SD. 57751

Brookside Motel
3 blocks east of traffic signal on State
Hwy. 40
Kitchens, pool, air conditioning
(605)666-4496
Box 137, Keystone, SD. 57751

Cloud 9 Motel
East of stop sign on State Hwy 40
(605)666-4607
Keystone, SD. 57751

Elk Haven Resort
South of Mt. Rushmore on U.S. Hwy. 16A
Cabins, Laundromat, groceries
(605)666-4856
Box 717, Keystone, SD. 57751

The First Lady Motel
U.S. Hwy. 16A, next to Keystone Mall
Facilities accessible to handicapped visitors, family rates
(605)666-4990
Keystone, SD. 57751

Kelly Inn
Facilities accessible to handicapped visitors, deluxe suites, family rooms, sauna, whirlpool, restaurants nearby
(605)666-4483 or (800)635-3559
Box 654, Keystone, SD. 57751

Miner's Motel
South of Keystone on U.S. Hwy. 16A
Heated pool, air conditioning, Laundromat, restaurant, store
(605)666-4638 or (800)843-1300, ext. 2600
Box 157, Keystone, SD. 57751

Powder House Lodge
(605)666-4646
Keystone, SD. 57751

Rushmore Manor Inn
Junction of U.S. Hwy. 16A and Swanzey St.
Heated pool, air conditioning
(605)666-4443 or (800)843-1300, ext. 3333
Keystone, SD. 57751

Rushmore View Motor Lodge
AAA, restaurant, no pets
(605)666-4466 or (800)888-2603
Keystone, SD. 57751

Spokane Creek Resort
10 miles south of Keystone on U.S. Hwy. 16A

Cabins with kitchenettes, heated pool, cafe, laundry, groups welcome
(605)666-4609
Box 313, Keystone, SD. 57751

Wagon Wheel Motel
Full hookups, air conditioning, rates by the day or week
(605)666-4426 or (605)666-4477
HCR 33, Box 91, Keystone, SD. 57751

Pactola Lodging

Black Hills Mountain Resort
2 miles south of Pactola Lake on U.S. Hwy. 385
Chalets with 1–4 bedrooms
(605)574-2985
HCR 33, Box 3113, Rapid City, SD. 57702

Rapid City Lodging

Alex Johnson Hotel
523 6th St.
Facilities accessible to handicapped visitors; single, double, and family rooms; full-service restaurant
(605)342-1210 or (800)843-8800
Rapid City, SD. 57701

Amber Inn
2018 Mt. Rushmore Rd.
Family rooms, kitchen units, air conditioning, play area, restaurants nearby
(605)343-3630 or (800)325-3389
Rapid City, SD. 57701

Anemarie's Country Bunny Bed and Breakfast
6 miles west of Rapid City on State Hwy. 44
Suite with private entrance, private bath, hot tub
(605)343-9234
RR 8, Box 840, Rapid City, SD. 57702

Audrie's Cranbury Corner Bed and Breakfast

7 miles west of Rapid City on State
    Hwy. 44
Antique furnishings, private
    entrance, private bath, couples
    only, no pets
(605)342-7788
RR 8, Box 2400, Rapid City, SD.
    57702

Avanti Inn
102 N. Maple
I-90, exit 57 or 60
Facilities accessible to handicapped
    visitors, kitchenettes, water beds,
    air conditioning, free continental
    breakfast
(605)348-1112 or (800)658-5464
Rapid City, SD. 57701

Bed and Breakfast H-D Lodge
7 miles west of Rapid City on State
    Hwy. 44
Private entrances, private baths,
    continental breakfast
(605)341-7580
RR 8, Box 3360, Rapid City, SD.
    57702

Bel Air Budget Host Inn
2101 Mt. Rushmore Rd.
AAA, air conditioning, family units,
    heated pool, restaurants nearby
(605)343-5126 or (800)283-4678
Rapid City, SD. 57701

Best Western Gill's Sun Inn
1901 W. Main St.
Restaurant, heated pool, air
    conditioning
(605)343-6040 or (800)528-123
Rapid City, SD. 577014

Best Western Town 'n Country Inn
2505 Mt. Rushmore Rd.
2 heated pools, playground, air
    conditioning, restaurant adjacent,
    no pets
(605)343-5383 or (800)528-1234
Rapid City, SD. 57701

Big Sky Motel
1 mile south of Rapid City on U.S.
Hwy. 16W
Singles, doubles, and family units, all
    ground level
(605)348-3200
Rapid City, SD. 57701

Black Forest Bed and Breakfast
    Lodge
2 miles south of Pactola Lake on U.S.
    Hwy. 385
Private baths, hot tubs
(605)574-2000 or (800)888-1607
HC 33, Box 3123, Rapid City, SD.
    57702

Budget Inn Motel
610 E. North St.
Facilities accessible to handicapped
    visitors, some kitchens, air
    conditioning, cafe close-by
(605)342-8594
Rapid City, SD. 57701

Carriage House Bed and Breakfast
721 West Blvd.
Antique furnishings, adults, no pets
(605)343-6415
Rapid City, SD. 57701

Castle Inn
15 E. North St.
Efficiencies, air conditioning, heated
    pool, restaurant adjoining
(605)348-4120 or (800)658-5464
Rapid City, SD. 57701

College Inn Motel
123 Kansas City St.
Facilities accessible to handicapped
    visitors, air conditioning, laundry,
    heated pool, restaurant adjoining
(800)742-8942 (South Dakota only)
    or (800)843-8892
Rapid City, SD. 57701

Colonial Motel
511 E. North St.
1-, 2-, or 3-bed units, air
    conditioning, pool
(605)342-1417
Rapid City, SD. 57701

Corral Motel
Air conditioning, restaurants close-
by
210 E. North St.
(605)342-7511

Dakota Motel
220 E. St. Joseph St.
Air conditioning, kitchenettes,
heated pool
(605)342-2896
Rapid City, SD. 57701

Days Inn Rapid City
125 Main St.
Facilities accessible to handicapped
visitors, restaurant, coffee shop,
pool
(605)343-5501 or (800)325-2525
Rapid City, SD. 57701

Econo Lodge of Rapid City
625 E. Disk Dr.
Facilities accessible to handicapped
visitors, heated pool, restaurant,
laundry
(605)342-6400 or (800)456-1064
Rapid City, SD. 57701

Fair Value Inn
I-90, exit 59 (LaCrosse St.)
Facilities accessible to handicapped
visitors, AAA, air conditioning
(605)342-8118
Rapid City, SD. 57701

Fantasy Inn
3737 Sturgis Rd.
Facilities accessible to handicapped
visitors, air conditioning, heated
pool, restaurant close-by
(605)342-2892
Rapid City, SD. 57702

Foothills Inn
I-90, exit 59 (LaCrosse St.)
Facilities accessible to handicapped
visitors, air conditioning, heated
pool, restaurant next-door
(605)348-5640
Rapid City, SD. 57701

Four Seasons Motel
930 E. North St.
Facilities accessible to handicapped
visitors, air conditioning,
kitchenettes, pool
(605)343-7822
Rapid City, SD. 57701

Golden Hills Motel
206 Main St.
Some kitchenettes, air conditioning
(605)342-6232
Rapid City, SD. 57701

Happy Holiday Motel
I-90, exit 57, 9 miles south on U.S.
Hwy. 16
Facilities accessible to handicapped
visitors; single, double, and family
units; air conditioning
(605)342-8101
HC 33, Box 8905, Rapid City, SD.
57701

Hillside Country Cottages
6 miles from Mt. Rushmore on U.S.
Hwy. 16
Cabins with kitchenettes, air
conditioning, laundry, playground
(605)342-4121
HC 33, Box 1901, Rapid City, SD.
57702

Holiday Inn Rapid City
I-90, exit 59 (LaCrosse St.)
(800)465-4329
Rapid City, SD. 57701

Holiday Inn Rushmore Plaza
I-90, exit 57, next to civic center
Facilities accessible to handicapped
visitors, indoor pool, sauna, air
conditioning, restaurant
(605)348-4000 or (800)777-1023
Rapid City, SD. 57701

Howard Johnson Motor Lodge
I-90, exit 59 (LaCrosse St.)
Facilities accessible to handicapped
visitors, indoor-outdoor pool,
Jacuzzi, sauna, steam room,

34

restaurant
(605)343-8550 or (800)654-2000
Rapid City, SD. 57701

Imperial Inn
125 Main St.
(605)343-5501 or (800)351-1477
Rapid City, SD. 57701

King X Lodge
I-90, exit 60, to State Hwy. 44W
AAA; suites with kitchens; single,
    double, and family units; air
    conditioning
(605)342-2236
Rapid City, SD. 57701

Lake Park Motel
State Hwy. 44W and Chapel Ln.
Family cottages, efficiencies, heated
    pool
(605)343-0234
Rt. 11, Box 1500, Rapid City, SD.
    57702

The Lamplighter Inn
27 St. Joseph St.
AAA, air conditioning, heated pool,
    family plan
(605)342-3385 or (800)347-6111
Rapid City, SD. 57701

Lazy U Motel
2215 Mt. Rushmore Rd.
Facilities accessible to handicapped
    visitors, AAA, family units, air
    conditioning, restaurant next-door
(605)343-4242
Rapid City, SD. 57701

Motel Rapid
3515 Sturgis Rd.
Facilities accessible to handicapped
    visitors, some apartment-size
    units, kitchenettes, air
    conditioning, pool
605)342-5834
Rapid City, SD. 57702

Plaza Sands Motel
212 East Blvd.

Air conditioning, heated pool
(605)343-8232 or (800)658-3986
Rapid City, SD. 57701

Quality Inn
2208 Mt. Rushmore Rd.
Air conditioning, 2 swimming pools,
    restaurant
(605)342-3322 or (800)221-2222
Rapid City, SD. 57701

Ramada Inn Rapid City
I-90, exit 59 (LaCrosse St.)
Facilities accessible to handicapped
    visitors, air conditioning, indoor
    pool with water slide, 24-hour
    restaurant
(605)342-1300 or (800)228-2828
Rapid City, SD. 57701

Rockerville Trading Post and Motel
U.S. Hwy. 16, between Rapid City
    and Mt. Rushmore
AAA, restaurant, pool, air
    conditioning, groceries, laundry,
    playground
(605)341-4880
HC 33, Box 1607, Rapid City, SD.
    57701

Rushmore Inn
5410 S. Mt. Rushmore Rd.
(605)343-4700
Rapid City, SD. 57701

Rushmore Motel
I-90, exit 59, S. to 1313 LaCrosse St.
AAA, air conditioning, restaurants
    close-by
(605)348-3313 or (800)256-3339
Rapid City, SD. 57701

Rushmore Plaza Motel
601 E. North St.
Kitchenettes and some family rooms,
    pool, air conditioning
(605)348-5080
Rapid City, SD. 57701

Sands of the Black Hills
2401 Mt. Rushmore Rd.

Some family units, air conditioning,
   pool
(605)348-1454
Rapid City, SD. 57701

Stables Motel
518 E. Omaha
LaCrosse St. and State Hwy. 44E
AAA, some family units, air
   conditioning, heated pool,
   Laundromat, ground-floor units
(605)342-9241
Rapid City, SD. 57701

Stardust Motel
520 E. North St.
Singles, doubles, suites, kitchenettes,
   air conditioning, heated pool,
   restaurants nearby
(605)343-8844 or (800)456-0084
Rapid City, SD. 57701

Super 8 Motel
I-90, exit 59, 2124 LaCrosse St.
Facilities accessible to handicapped
   visitors, air conditioning, 24-hour
   restaurant
(605)348-8070 or (800)800-8000
Rapid City, SD. 57701

Super 8 Motel
2520 Mt. Rushmore Rd.
(605)342-4911 or (800)800-8000
Rapid City, SD. 57701

Thrifty Motor Inn
I-90, Exit 59 (LaCrosse St)
Facilities accessible to handicapped
   visitors, air conditioning, large
   units
(605)342-0551
Rapid City, SD. 57701

Tip Top Motor Hotel
405 St. Joseph St.
AAA, pool, laundry
(605)343-3901 or (800)341-8000
Rapid City, SD. 57701

Town House Motel
2nd St. and St. Joseph St.

AAA, air conditioning, heated pool,
   no pets
(605)342-8143 or (800)843-1300
Rapid City, SD. 57701

Trade Winds Motel
420 E. North St.
Facilities accessible to handicapped
   visitors, kitchenettes, air
   conditioning, heated pool
(605)342-4153
Rapid City, SD. 57701

Rockerville Lodging
Gold Nugget Motel
10 miles northeast of Mt. Rushmore
   on U.S. Hwy. 16
AAA, air conditioning, playground,
   heated pool
(605)348-2082
HCR 33, Box 1605, Rapid City, SD.
   57701

Spearfish Lodging
Antler Motel
517 W. Jackson Blvd.
I-90, exit 12
Air conditioning, heated pool, hot
   tub, water beds
(605)642-5753
Spearfish, SD. 57783

Bell's Motor Lodge
230 Main St.
Kitchen and family units, air
   conditioning, heated pool,
   playground
(605)642-2754
Spearfish, SD. 57783

Best Western of Spearfish
I-90, exit 14
Facilities accessible to handicapped
   visitors, AAA, air conditioning,
   laundry, restaurant, videocassette
   recorder with remote in every
   room, indoor pool, 2 Jacuzzis
(605)642-8105 or (800)528-1234
PO Box 576, Spearfish, SD. 57783

Best Western Sundown Motel
346 W. Kansas
I-90, exit 12
AAA, indoor pool, saunas,
 whirlpool, laundry, restaurants
 nearby
(605)642-4676 or (800)528-1234
Spearfish, SD. 57783

Canyon Gateway Motel
1/2 mile into Spearfish Canyon on
 U.S. Hwy. 14A
(605)642-3402
Spearfish, SD. 57783

Capp Motel
333 W. Jackson Blvd.
I-90, exit 12
Cabins with kitchens, air
 conditioning
(605)642-3611
Spearfish, SD. 57783

Christensen's Country Home Bed
 and Breakfast
432 Hillsview
(605)642-2859
Spearfish, SD. 57783

Days Inn
240 Ryan Rd.
Suites available, Jacuzzis, sauna
(605)642-7101
Spearfish, SD. 57783

Hilltop Motel
I-90, exit 14, 211 Main St.
(605)642-7105
Spearfish, SD. 57783

Holiday Inn of the Northern Black
 Hills
I-90, exit 14
(605)642-4683
Spearfish, SD. 57783

Kelly Inn
540 E. Jackson Blvd.
I-90, exit 12
Facilities accessible to handicapped
 visitors, whirlpool, sauna, laundry,

restaurant next-door
(605)642-7795 or (800)635-3559
Spearfish, SD. 57783

Kozy Motel
427 Main St.
Facilities accessible to handicapped
 visitors, at-door parking, air
 conditioning, downtown cafes
 close-by
(605)642-4846
Spearfish, SD. 57783

L-Rancho Motel
334 W. Jackson Blvd.
I-90, exit 12
Kitchenettes, air conditioning,
 heated pool, hot tub, pets
 welcome
(605)642-2061
Spearfish, SD. 57783

Queens Motel
305 Main St.
AAA, at-door parking, air
 conditioning, downtown cafes
 close-by
(605)642-2631
Spearfish, SD. 57783

Rimlock Lodge
In Spearfish Canyon, U.S. Hwy 14A
Cabins
(605)642-3192
Spearfish, SD. 57783

Royal Rest Motel
444 Main St.
AAA, heated pool, air conditioning,
 restaurants close-by
(605)642-3842
Spearfish, SD. 57783

Shady Pines Cabins and Motel
514 Mason
Cabins for cooking (no utensils), air
 conditioning
(605)642-9909 or (605)642-4234
Spearfish, SD. 57783

Sherwood Lodge
231 W. Jackson Blvd.

I-90, exit 12
Restaurants close-by
(605)642-4688 or (800)234-2032
Spearfish, SD. 57783

Spearfish Canyon Lodge
In Spearfish Canyon, U.S. Hwy. 14A
Cabins
(605)584-3027
Spearfish, SD. 57783

Spearfish Creek Inn
430 W. Kansas
Some kitchens, air conditioning,
   heated pool, restaurants close-by
(605)642-9941
Spearfish, SD. 57783

Super 8 Motel
Heritage Dr.
I-90, exit 14
(605)642-4721 or (800)800-8000
Spearfish, SD. 57783

Belle Fourche Lodging

La Belle Motel
Junction of U.S. Hwy. 85 and State
   Hwy. 34
Air conditioning, at-room parking,
   24-hour restaurant next-door,
   ample truck parking
(605)892-2634
Belle Fourche, SD. 57717

Motel Lariat
1033 Elkhorn St.
East of downtown Belle Fourche on
   Hwy. 212
Air conditioning, pets welcome, at-
   door parking
(605)892-2601
Belle Fourche, SD. 57717

Super 8 Motel
501 National St.
(605)892-3361 or (800)800-8000
Belle Fourche, SD. 57717

Custer Lodging

All American Inn
437 Montgomery St.
Air conditioning, heated pool and

spa, free access to facilities at
American President's Resort, 10
percent off if reserved by June 1
(605)673-4051
Custer, SD. 57730

Allen's Rocket Motel
211 Mt. Rushmore Rd.
U.S. Hwys. 16 and 385
Family units, air conditioning,
   restaurants and shops close-by
(605)673-4401
Custer, SD. 57730

American President's Motel, Cabins
   and Camp
1 mile east of Custer on U.S. Hwy.
   16A
Heated pool, spa, air conditioning,
   10 percent off if reserved by May
   15
(605)673-3373
PO Box 46, Custer, SD. 57730

Bavarian Inn
U.S. Hwy. 16/385
AAA, air conditioning, 1- and
   2-room suites, indoor pool, sauna,
   playground, restaurant
(605)673-2802 or (800)657-4312
PO Box 152, Custer, SD. 57730

Buzzard's Roost Cottages
1 mile east of Custer on U.S. Hwy.
   16A
Completely furnished kitchenettes
   and cottages, air conditioning
(605)673-2326
Custer, SD. 57730

Chalet Motel
933 Mt. Rushmore Road, U.S. Hwy.
   16A east
Air conditioning; 1-, 2-, and 3-bed
   units; kitchenettes; some cabins;
   at-door parking
(605)673-2393 or (800)843-1300
Custer, SD. 57730

Chief Motel
120 Mt. Rushmore Road, U.S. Hwy.
   16W

AAA; indoor pool; spa; restaurant;
1-, 2-, and 3-bed units
(605)673-2318
Custer, SD. 57730

Custer Mansion Bed and Breakfast
325 Centennial Dr.
1891 Victorian-Gothic home,
children welcome, no smoking or
pets
(605)673-3333
Custer, SD. 57730

The Custer Motel
109 Mt. Rushmore Rd.
AAA, heated pool, air conditioning,
10 percent off if reserved by June 1
(605)673-2876
Custer, SD. 57730

Dakota Cowboy Inn
AAA; heated pool; playground; air
conditioning; 1-, 2-, and 3-bed
units to accommodate 1–8
persons; special 3-day rates
(605)673-4659
Custer, SD. 57730

French Creek Inn Motel
932 Mt. Rushmore Rd.
Air conditioning, free access to
facilities at American President's
Resort, 10 percent off if reserved
by June 1
(605)673-3003
Custer, SD. 57730

Hi Ho Best Western
Restaurant, heated pool, sauna,
playground
(605)673-2275
PO Box 568, Custer, SD. 57730

Mile Hi Motel
244 Mt. Rushmore Rd.
Family units, restaurant next-door
(605)673-4048
Custer, SD. 57730

Rock Crest Lodge
AAA, at-door parking, air

conditioning, family units,
restaurants close-by
(605)673-4323
PO Box 687, Custer, SD. 57730

Shady Rest Motel
1½ blocks south and west of Court
House Museum
Cabins in pines, pool, family units,
kitchenettes, air conditioning,
baby sitting
(605)673-4478
Custer, SD. 57730

Sun-Mark Inn
342 Mt. Rushmore Rd.
Facilities accessible to handicapped
visitors, spa, restaurants close-by
(605)673-4400 or (800)351-1477
Custer, SD. 57730

Sunset Motel
525 Crook St., U.S. Hwy. 16/385
Facilities accessible to handicapped
visitors, at-door parking, pool, air
conditioning, restaurants 1 block
away
(605)673-2821
Custer, SD. 57730

Super 8 Motel
West of Custer
(605)673-2200 or (800)800-8000
Custer, SD. 57730

Valley Motel
1 mile east of Custer on U.S. Hwy.
16A
1- and 2-bedroom units, air
conditioning, kitchenettes
available, playground
(605)673-4819
Custer, SD. 57730

Western Star Motel
905 Mt. Rushmore Rd.
U.S. Hwy. 16A
Family units, air conditioning,
heated pool, restaurants close-by
(605)673-4145 or (800)351-1477
Custer, SD. 57730

Custer State Park Lodging

Blue Bell Lodge and Resort
State Hwy. 87S, in park
Facilities accessible to handicapped
visitors, secluded cabins, home-
cooked meals and cookouts,
general store
(605)255-4531 or (800)658-3530
HCR 83, Box 63, Custer, SD. 57730

Legion Lake Resort
At central location in park
Facilities accessible to handicapped
visitors, cottages, 2- and 3-room
housekeeping units, restaurant
(605)255-4521 or (800)658-3530
HCR 83, Box 67, Custer, SD. 57730

Spokane Creek Resort
10 miles south of Keystone on U.S.
Hwy. 16A, on edge of park
Facilities accessible to handicapped
visitors, cabins, kitchenettes, cafe,
store, heated pool, playground,
laundry
(605)666-4609
Box 313, Keystone, SD. 57751

State Game Lodge Resort
Facilities accessible to handicapped
visitors, rooms in lodge, motel
units, cottages, restaurant
(605)255-4541 or (800)658-3530
HCR 83, Box 74, Custer, SD. 57730

Sylvan Lake Lodge and Resort
At intersection of State Hwys. 87 and
89
Facilities accessible to handicapped
visitors, cabins and cottages with
kitchenettes, restaurant
(605)574-2561
Box 752, Custer, SD. 57730

Hot Springs Lodging

Battle Mountain Motel
402 Battle Mountain Ave.
U.S. Hwy. 385 and State Hwy. 87N
Air conditioning, cafes nearby
(605)745-3182
Hot Springs, SD. 57747

Best Western Inn by the River
Downtown Hot Springs on U.S.
Hwy. 385
(605)745-4292 or (800)528-1234

Bison Motel
South of downtown Hot Springs on
U.S. Hwy. 385
Family and single units, kitchens, air
conditioning, restaurants close-by
(605)745-5191
Hot Springs, SD. 57747

Black Hills Motel
West of Hot Springs on Hwy. 18
Singles, divided doubles, family
units, air conditioning
(605)745-5873
Hot Springs, SD. 57747

Cascade Ranch Bed and Breakfast
9 miles south of Hot Springs on State
Hwy. 71
2-bedroom western ranch house
with private bath
(605)745-3397
PO Box 461, Hot Springs, SD. 57747

El Rancho Motel
640 S. 6th St.
AAA, heated pool, restaurants close-
by
(605)745-3130 or (800)341-8000
Hot Springs, SD. 57747

Super 8 Motel
800 Mammoth St.
Facilities accessible to handicapped
visitors, full-service restaurant
(605)745-3888 or (800)848-8888
PO Box 612, Hot Springs, SD. 57747

Villa Theresa Guest House
801 Almond St.
Bed and breakfast in 1893 home, 4
bedrooms with private bath, no
smoking or pets, children
welcome
(605)745-4633
Hot Springs, SD. 57747

Wayside Motel
510 S. 6th St., S. Hot Springs on State
    Hwy. 87 and U.S. Hwys. 18/385
Family and single units, air
    conditioning
(605)745-3199
Hot Springs, SD. 57747

Kadoka Lodging

Best Western H&H El Centro Motel
I-90, exit 150 or 152
Facilities accessible to handicapped
    visitors, AAA, spa, laundry, air
    conditioning, heated pool,
    playground, restaurant
(605)837-2287 or (800)528-1234
Kadoka, SD. 57543

Cuckleburr Motel
I-90, exit 150
Air conditioning, heated pool, pets,
    continental breakfast
(605)837-2151, (800)323-7988, or
    (800)341-8000
Kadoka, SD. 57543

Hill Top Motel
I-90, exits 150 and 152
Air conditioning, restaurants close-
    by
(605)837-2216
PO Box 543, Kadoka, SD. 57543

Leewood Motel
I-90, exit 150
Facilities accessible to handicapped
    visitors, pool
(605)837-2238
PO Box 461, Kadoka, SD. 57543

Ponderosa Motel
I-90, between exits 150 and 152
Facilities accessible to handicapped
    visitors, AAA, singles, doubles,
    heated pool, hot tub, Laundromat
(605)837-2362
Box 64, Kadoka, SD. 57543

Sundowner Motor Inn
I-90, exit 150
AAA, restaurant, air conditioning,
    extra-long beds, heated pool

(605)837-2296 or (800)432-5682
Kadoka, SD. 57543

Wagon Wheel Motel
I-90, exit 150
Facilities accessible to handicapped
    visitors, air conditioning, cooking
    facilities, cafe ½ block away
(605)837-2404
Kadoka, SD. 57543

West Motel
I-90, exit 150 or 152
AAA, air conditioning, restaurants
    within walking distance
(605)837-2427
Box 247, Kadoka, SD. 57543

Wall Lodging

Best Western Plains Motel
712 Glenn
AAA, family units, air conditioning,
    restaurants close-by
(605)279-2145 or (800)528-1234
Wall, SD. 57790

Elk Motel and Restaurant
Junction of I-90 and State Hwy. 240
Facilities accessible to handicapped
    visitors, AAA, some water beds, air
    conditioning, restaurant, heated
    pool, Laundromat
(605)279-2127 or (800)782-9402
Wall, SD. 57790

Fountain Motel
I-90, exit 109 or 110
Air conditioning, restaurant next-
    door
(605)279-2488
Wall, SD. 57790

Hillcrest Motel
Facilities accessible to handicapped
    visitors, cottages, kitchenettes, air
    conditioning, playground
(605)279-2415 or (800)888-1326
Box 321, Wall, SD. 57790

Hitching Post Motel
I-90, exit 110, 10th Ave.

AAA, air conditioning, heated pool,
  playground, restaurant opposite
(605)279-2133
Wall, SD. 57790

King's Inn
608 Main St.
Facilities accessible to handicapped
  visitors, AAA, heated pool, air
  conditioning, restaurants close-by
(605)279-2178 or (800)782-2613
PO Box 440, Wall, SD. 57790

Sands Motor Inn
I-90, exit 110
Facilities accessible to handicapped
  visitors, AAA, heated pool, air
  conditioning, restaurants close-by
(605)279-2121 or (800)341-8000
Wall, SD. 57790

Super 8 Motel
I-90, exit 110, 711 Glenn St.
Facilities accessible to handicapped
  visitors, extra-long beds, air
  conditioning, restaurants close-by
(605)279-2688 or (800)800-8000
Box 426, Wall, SD. 57790

Wall Motel
I-90, exit 110
Facilities accessible to handicapped
  visitors, ground-level rooms, air
  conditioning, restaurants close-by
(605)279-2624
Wall, SD. 57790

Welsh's Motel
3-bed connecting units, air
  conditioning
(605)279-2271
Wall, SD. 57790

Badlands National Park
Badlands Budget Host Motel
I-90, exit 131, south to State Hwy. 44
Pool, air conditioning, playground,
  groceries, laundry
(605)433-5335, (800)283-4678, or
  (800)999-6116
HC 54, Box 115, Interior, SD. 57750

Cedar Pass Lodge
I-90, exit 131, 8 miles south
AAA, air conditioning cabins,
  restaurant
(605)433-5460
Box 5, Interior, SD. 57750

Prairie's Edge Bed and Breakfast
I-90, exit 131, 1 1/2 miles south of
  Interior
No children under 4, no pets
(605)433-5441 or (605)456-2836
PO Box 11, Interior, SD. 57750

Sundance, Wyoming, Lodging
Best Western Inn at Sundance
(307)283-2800 or (800)528-1234
Sundance, WY. 82729

Restaurants

Custer Restaurants
Bavarian Restaurant
U.S. Hwys. 16/385
German and American food, full
  service
(605)673-4412

The Chief Restaurant
140 Mt. Rushmore Rd.
U.S. Hwy. 16W
American food, full service
(605)673-4402

Dairy Queen of Custer County
335 Mt. Rushmore Rd.
U.S. Hwy. 16
American fast food
(605)673-2194

The Fort
3 miles north of Custer on U.S. Hwy.
  16/385
American food, full service, facilities
  accessible to handicapped visitors
(605)673-4761

Skyway Restaurant Lounge
511 Mt. Rushmore Rd.
American food, full service
(605)673-4477

Custer State Park Restaurants

Battle Creek Station
12 miles south of Rapid City on State
    Hwy. 79
American food, full service, facilities
    accessible to handicapped visitors
(605)255-4555

Blue Bell Lodge and Resort
Custer State Park
American food, full service, facilities
    accessible to handicapped visitors
(605)255-4531

Coolidge Inn
Near State Game Lodge, U.S. Hwy.
    16A, Custer State Park
American food, cafeteria, facilities
    accessible to handicapped visitors
(605)255-4541

Legion Lake Resort
American food, full service, facilities
    accessible to handicapped visitors
(605)255-4521

State Game Lodge
American food, full service, facilities
    accessible to handicapped visitors
(605)255-4541

Sylvan Lake Lodge
Junction of State Hwys. 87 and 89
American food, full service, facilities
    accessible to handicapped visitors
(605)574-2561

Deadwood Restaurants

Bodega Bar and Cafe
662 Main St.
American food, full service
(605)578-1996 or 578-2055

Cousin Jacks
607 Main St.
American food, full service
(605)578-2036

The Depot
155 Sherman St.
American food, full service
(605)578-2699

Faro's Restaurant
700 Main St.
American food, full service
(605)578-1465

Gold Dust
688 Main St.
American food, buffet
(605)578-2100

Marcille's
620 Main St.
American food, full service
(605)578-3060

Midnight Star
677 Main St.
American food, full service
(605)578-1555

Silverado
709 Main St.
American food, full service
(605)578-3670

Hill City Restaurants

Alpine Inn
On Main St. in Harney Peak Hotel
American food, full service
(605)574-2749

Best Western Golden Spike Inn and
    Restaurant
U.S. Hwys. 16/385
American food, full service
(605)574-2577

Kadoka Restaurants

Denni's Texaco/Cafe I-90, exit 150
American food, full service
(605)837-2801

H&H El Centro Restaurant and
    Coffee Shop
I-90, exit 150 or 152
American food, full service
(605)837-2265

Nibble Nook Drive Inn
I-90, exit 150, on W. Kadoka
American fast food
(605)837-2138

Keystone Restaurants

Mount Rushmore
American food, full service
(605)574-2515

Ruby House Restaurant and Red
  Garter Saloon
Downtown Keystone
American food, full service
(605)666-4404

Piedmont
Elk Creek Steakhouse and Lounge
I-90, exit 46
American food, full service
(605)787-6349

Sacora Station Restaurant
I-90, between exits 46 and 48
American food, full service
(605)787-4154

Rapid City Restaurants

Arby's
535 Mountain View
American fast food
(605)341-4540

Arby's
Rushmore Mall
American fast food
(605)341-6022

B. J. Grinder King
902 Main St.
Pizza and sandwiches, fast food
(605)348-3166

Bodega II
3939 Canyon Lake Dr.
Italian food, full service
(605)348-7432

Bonanza Sirloin Pit
1118 E. North St.
American food, buffet
(605)342-7484

Burger King
515 Mountain View
American fast food
(605)348-3888

Burger King
1002 E. North St.
American fast food
(605)348-2450

Canyon Lake Supper Club
4205 Jackson Blvd.
American food, full service
(605)348-5739

Casa Del Rey
1902 Mt. Rushmore Rd.
Mexican-American food, full service
(605)348-5679

CG's
Rushmore Mall
Italian-American food, full service
(605)348-0988

Chef Rudy's Family Restaurant
1720 Mt. Rushmore Rd.
American food, full service
(605)348-6733

China Palace
2421 W. Main St.
Chinese food, full service
(605)348-4195

Chuckwagon
3609 Sturgis Rd.
American food, full service, buffet
(605)343-9375

Circle B Ranch
Keystone Rt.
Barbecue, buffet
(605)348-7358

Colonial House
2501 Mt. Rushmore Rd.
American food, full service
(605)342-4640

Copper Creek Food and Spirits
2424 W. Main St.
Continental food, full service
(605)348-3348

Dairy Queen
1702 Mt. Rushmore Rd.

American fast food
(605)342-4874

Dakota Family Restaurant
2601 N. Maple
American food, full service
(605)348-1756

Dakota House
815 E. North St.
American food, full service
(605)343-6541

Domino's Pizza
Baken Park–Creekside
American food, pizza delivery
(605)343-3400

Domino's Pizza
Ellsworth Air Force Base (AFB)
American food, pizza delivery
(605)934-1491

Domino's Pizza
903 E. North St.
American food, pizza delivery
(605)341-2401

Don Rafael's
725 Indiana
Mexican-American food, full service
(605)341-4118

Families Submarine Shop
333 6th St.
Gyros and submarine sandwiches,
   fast food
(605)343-7827

Family Thrift Center Delis
3333 W. Chicago
American fast food, buffet
(605)348-1377

Family Thrift Center Delis
1516 E. St. Patrick
American fast food, buffet
(605)343-4326

Flying T Chuckwagon Cowboy
   Supper and Show

6 miles south of Rapid City on U.S.
   Hwy. 16
Western food, buffet, facilities
   accessible to handicapped visitors
(605)342-1905

Gill's Sun Inn Restaurant
1901 W. Main St.
American food, full service
(605)343-6040

Great Wall Chinese Restaurant
315 E. North St.
Chinese food, full service
(605)348-1060

Happy Chef
2110 LaCrosse St.
American food, full service
(605)348-6898

Happy Chef
2121 W. Main St.
American food, full service
(605)348-6667

Happy Joe's Pizza and Ice Cream
   Parlor
211 Cambell
Italian-American food, buffet
(605)348-5343

Hara's
Rushmore Mall
American food, full service
(605)348-0944

Hardee's
5th and St. Joseph St.
American fast food
(605)348-5692

Hardee's
1001 E. North St.
American fast food
(605)342-6864

Hardee's
Rushmore Mall
American fast food
(605)342-7155

Harold's Prime Rib
318 East Blvd.
American food, full service
(605)343-1927

JB's Big Boy Restaurant
801 Mt. Rushmore Rd.
American food, full service
(605)348-2460

JB's Big Boy Restaurant
717 E. North St.
American food, full service
(605)343-4203

Bar and Grill
701 St. Joseph St.
American food, full service
(605)343-6402

Kentucky Fried Chicken
1918 W. Main St.
American fast food
(605)342-1515

Kentucky Fried Chicken
918 E. North St.
American fast food
(605)342-2515

Supper Club
1981 E. Centre St.
American food, full service
(605)343-3328

McDonald's
720 Cleveland
American fast food
(605)343-6984

McDonald's
2223 W. Main St.
American fast food
(605)342-3483

McDonald's
804 E. North St.
American fast food
(605)342-3772

Millstone
2010 W. Main St.

American food, full service
(605)343-5824

Missing Link
523 Main St.
European food, full deli
(605)348-8385

Mr. Steak
2125 Haynes
American food, full service
(605)342-1543

Murphy's Prime Rib and Deli
510 9th St.
American food, full service
(605)348-7270

1915 Firehouse
610 Main St.
Continental food, full service
(605)348-1915

Parkway Restaurant
312 East Blvd. N
American food, full service
(605)342-9640

Perkins
1715 LaCrosse St.
American food, full service
(605)341-3810

Perkins
2305 Mt. Rushmore Rd.
American food, full service
(605)341-5225

Pizza Hut
Ellsworth AFB
Pizza, full service and take-out
(605)923-5832

Pizza Hut
2604 W. Main St.
Pizza, full service and take-out
(605)343-1511

Pizza Hut
2005 Mt. Rushmore Rd.
Pizza, full service and take-out
(605)342-1542

Pizza Hut
705 E. North St.
Pizza, full service and take-out
(605)341-4211

Royal Fork Buffet
160 Disk Dr.
American food, buffet
(605)342-9166

Shakey's Pizza
720 Indiana
American fast food, buffet
(605)343-7228

Shooters
2424 W. Main St.
Outdoor beer garden, fast food
(605)348-3348

620 Main Street
620 Main St.
European food, full service
(605)343-2272

Smiley's Pizza Plus
418 E. St. Joseph St.
Indian tacos and pizza, fast food
(605)341-6180

Taco Bell
2323 W. Main St.
Mexican fast food
(605)341-5202

Taco Bell
902 E. North St.
Mexican fast food
(605)341-7564

Taco John's
1710 Cambell
American fast food
(605)343-6778

Taco John's
3020 W. Main St.
American fast food
(605)343-6432

Tally's Restaurant
530 6th St.

American food, full service
(605)342-7621

TCBY—The Country's Best Yogurt
2218 Jackson Blvd.
American fast food
(605)342-7020

Tip Top Restaurant
405 St. Joseph St.
American food, buffet
(605)343-3901

Wendy's Hamburgers
520 Mountain View Rd.
American fast food
(605)342-2220

Wendy's Hamburgers
701 E. North St.
American fast food
(605)343-9333

Windmill Restaurant
I-90, exit 55
American food, full service and
    buffet
(605)348-7072

Rockerville Restaurants
The Gaslight Restaurant
10 miles south of Rapid City on U.S.
    Hwy. 16
American food, full service, facilities
    accessible to handicapped visitors
(605)343-9276

Spearfish Restaurants
Bell Steakhouse and Firewater
    Lounge
539 W. Jackson Blvd.
American food, full service
(605)642-2848

Burger King
123 E. Utah Blvd.
American fast food
(605)642-4332

Cedar House Restaurant
130 E. Ryan Rd.

American food, full service
(605)642-2104

Claim #2
Corner of Main St. and Jackson Blvd.
American fast food
(605)642-1500

Country Kitchen
620 E. Jackson Blvd.
American food, full service
(605)642-4200

Dairy Queen
1912 North Ave.
American fast food
(605)642-2267

Domino's Pizza
1410 North Ave.
American food, pizza delivery
(605)642-2794

El Cocina
1410 North Ave.
Mexican and American food, full
    service
(605)642-3547

Golden Dragon
1850 North Ave.
Chinese and American food, full
    service
(605)642-2641

A Little Bit of Italy
447 Main St.
Italian and American food, full
    service
(605)642-5701

Lown House Garden Deli
745 5th St.
American food, full service
(605)642-5663

McDonald's
131 Ryan Rd.
American fast food
(605)642-2053

Margie's Dinner Club
83 U.S. Hwy. 14
American food, full service
(605)642-4765

Pizza Hut
435 W. Jackson Blvd.
American food, full service and take-
    out
(605)642-7717

Pizza Ranch
715 Main St.
American food, pizza delivery
(605)642-5947

Pok-A-Dots
228 W. Grant
American fast food
(605)642-3322

Sam's II
I-90, exit 14
American food, full service
(605)642-7357

Subway
1712 North Ave.
Submarine sandwiches, fast food
(605)642-5205

Taco John's
504 W. Jackson Blvd.
Mexican fast food
(605)642-4620

Valley Cafe
608 Main St.
American food, full service
(605)642-2423

Wendy's
220 Ryan Rd.
American fast food
(605)642-4037

Spearfish Canyon Restaurants
Cheyenne Crossing Cafe
U.S. Hwys. 14A and 85
American food, full service
(605)584-3510

48

Latchstring Restaurant
Between Deadwood and Spearfish
  on U.S. Hwy. 14A
American food, full service, facilities
  accessible to handicapped visitors
(605)584-3333

Sturgis Restaurants
Bob's Family Restaurant
1039 Main St.
American food, full service
(605)347-2930

McDonald's
2351 Lazelle St.
American fast food
(605)347-2798

Philtown Inn
American food, full service
(605)347-3604

Pizza Hut
American food, full service
(605)347-4573

Taco John's
Mexican fast food
(605)347-3556

Veterans Club
American food
(605)347-9938

Wall Restaurants
Cactus Restaurant and Lounge
I-90, exit 11
American food, full service
(605)279-2561

Dairy Queen
I-90, exit 110
American fast food, facilities
  accessible to handicapped visitors
(605)279-2655

Elkton House Restaurant
I-90, exit 110
American food, full service, facilities
  accessible to handicapped visitors
(605)279-2152

Wall Drug Store
510 Main St.
American food, full service, facilities
  accessible to handicapped visitors
(605)279-2175

Additional Information
For more information on camping, lodging, restaurants, and attractions in the Black Hills area, call the chambers of commerce in the individual communities or contact the state division of tourism.

Chambers of Commerce
Custer Chamber of Commerce
(800)992-9818

Hill City Chamber of Commerce
(800)888-1798

Keystone Chamber of Commerce
(800)843-1300, ext. 939

Sturgis Chamber of Commerce
  Information Center
(605)347-2556

Spearfish Chamber of Commerce
(800)626-8013

Wall Chamber of Commerce
(605)279-2665

State Division of Tourism
South Dakota Division of Tourism
Capitol Lake Plaza
Pierre, SD 57501
(800)843-1930

Chapter 4

Northern Hills Ride: Devils Tower

During rally week, a number of organized rides—or tours, as they are called—start from rally headquarters in Sturgis. A popular one is the Northern Hills Tour, which heads west from Sturgis into Wyoming. Movie buffs may already be familiar with the destination, Devils Tower, which was featured in the movie *Close Encounters of the Third Kind*. If you enjoy the companionship of others, by all means go on the tour, but this ride is enjoyable two up or even on your own. Traveling alone presents ample opportunities to meet new friends, since throughout rally week, hundreds of bikes will be going in whatever direction you decide to take.

Head northwest out of Sturgis along Interstate 90 into Wyoming and exit at U.S. Highway 14, again traveling northwest. Turn north at Devils Tower Junction and follow State Highway 24 right to the monument. You really don't need a map, since the route is well posted and well traveled.

Devils Tower, just over the state line in Wyoming, is an easy ride from Sturgis. As the rock contracted and fractured during cooling, pieces weighing hundreds of tons broke away to form a pile around the base. Falls still occur periodically. Devils Tower stands 867ft above its base and 5,117ft above sea level.

The tower formed when molten magma forced its way into sedimentary rock and then cooled underground. Over the course of several million years, the sedimentary rock eroded away and left a pillar of cooled magma rock exposed. In cooling, the rock contracted and fractured. Pieces hundreds of feet long, weighing thousands of tons, broke away and now form a giant rock pile around the base of the shaft.

Devils Tower is a favorite with rock climbers, and if you walk the easy trail, which circles the base, you may see some. The monument was first climbed on July Fourth in 1893 by two guys who built a ladder to scale the first 300 feet. In typical entrepreneurial style, their wives ran a refreshment stand and sold souvenirs to the more than 1,000 people assembled.

If you wish to stay overnight, the park has campsites available on a first-come, first-served basis. Water, johns, fireplaces, and tables are all nearby, and restaurants are within a couple of miles. But there are no showers. Big deal; so you don't shower for one day.

When heading back toward Sturgis and the Black Hills, travel north on State Highway 24 to Hulett. From Hulett, Highway 24 turns east toward Belle Fourche, and you'll find it a

Stepping into the general store in Aladdin, Wyoming, is like stepping back into time. Stop there and cool off with a sarsaparilla.

pleasant ride to the general store in Alladin, Wyoming. The store is the treasure one occasionally stumbles across, so plan on stopping in for a sarsaparilla.

From Alladin, continue east on State Highways 24 and 34 to Interstate 90 at Whitewood. Or head south at the junction of U.S. Route 85, and explore Spearfish before heading back to Sturgis.

Round trip mileage from Sturgis: About 160

Time required: Better part of a day

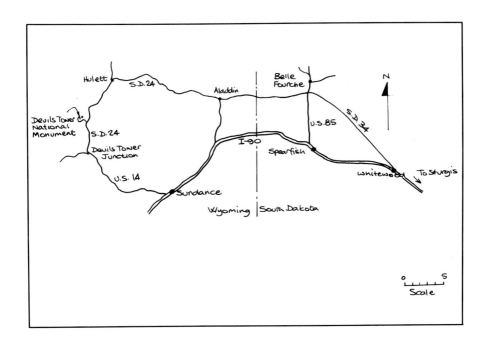

The Devils Tower is an easy ride from
Sturgis.

Chapter 5

Deadwood, Lead, and Spearfish Ride: Wild Bill, Calamity Jane, and Others

Fourteen miles from Sturgis, and one of the places you will undoubtedly visit, is the town that made the Black Hills famous: Deadwood. Deadwood Gulch, as it was originally known, was a gold rush town that grew up practically overnight. Its history is the stuff of the Old West, and with narrow streets, plus 100-year-old buildings, it has retained much of its frontier flavor.

James Butler ("Wild Bill") Hickok and Martha Jane ("Calamity Jane") Burke were synonymous with Deadwood during the town's gold rush days, but many other people also had unforgettable names, such as Potato Creek Johnny (John Perrett), Preacher Smith (Henry Weston Smith), Poker Alice (Alice Ivers), Deadwood Dick (Dick Brown), and Sheriff Seth Bullock. Much of the history of Deadwood can be found at the Adams Museum, where you get an idea of what it was really like to be a gold prospector during a Black Hills winter. The Adams is run by volunteers, and admission is free, but you might

Blue sky above, a twisting road below— and in between, 1,000ft-high limestone palisades dotted with Black Hills spruce trees. Spearfish Canyon is almost too good to be true.

want to put a couple of bucks in the jar by the door on your way out.

More of Deadwood's past rests in the Mount Mariah Cemetery, Deadwood's Boot Hill, perched atop the steep valley. A tour map of just who is buried there, and where, is available at the gate. Although touring a cemetery might seem bizarre to some, the walk amongst Mount Mariah's pines can be both informative and relaxing.

If you are looking down from the cemetery, Deadwood appears as an idyllic town nestled in a narrow valley. But all has not been well with Deadwood for some years. The town has very little room to expand, and very few jobs other than those associated with the tourist industry. In an effort to bring in much-needed money, Deadwood voters approved Las Vegas–style gambling, which began November 1, 1989. With a return to gambling some one hundred years later, Deadwood has once again become a boom town, but the prosperity has worsened an already-tight parking problem, especially during rally week, when thousands of us descend on the town each day. Motorcycle parking is not permitted on Main or on other nearby streets during rally week, and should you happen to miss the abundant No Parking signs, a ticket will cost you 100 big ones. By all means, drive your motor-

Yes, folks, here in Deadwood, the spirit of the Old West still lives! With the passage of a gambling ordinance, Deadwood has once again become a boom town. In the background is the Bella Union Theatre, where Wild Bill Hickok's killer, Jack Mc-Call, was tried for and acquitted of murder. McCall was acquitted because the court believed McCall had reason, since Hickok had previously killed McCall's brother, and because the court had no jurisdiction in Dakota Territory. McCall was tried a second time and hanged in Yankton, South Dakota, nine months later.

cycle up Deadwood's Main Street, but then turn left and park it in the large bike lot by the fire station.

From Mount Mariah, you can also see the Homestake Gold Mine 3 miles away in Lead. When the placer or alluvial deposits containing gold in particles large enough to be obtained by washing ran out, deep rock mining became the order of the day, and Homestake has become the largest operating gold mine in North America. The shafts go as deep as 8,000 feet, and the galleries spread out for miles under the hills.

Lead (pronounced *Leed*) isn't the prettiest town in the Black Hills, but you might want to check it out. After all, there can't be too many places where mining at the surface may eventually cut a town in two, as the Open Cut threatens to do here. Lead is a 5-minute ride from Deadwood; look for the signs.

When you leave Lead, head southwest toward Spearfish Canyon. The

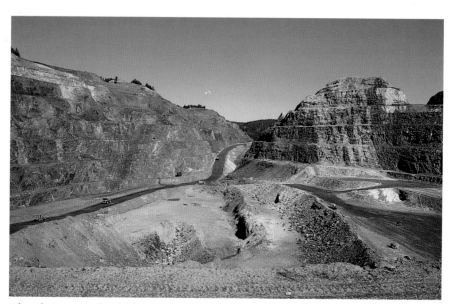

The discovery of gold-bearing ore, or "lead," in 1876 gave birth to the town of Lead. The Open Cut, as it is known, is part of the Homestake Mining's surface opera-tions, shown here in August 1990 and getting larger each year, threatens eventually to cut the town in half.

The largest operating gold mine in the United States, the Homestake Gold Mine produces over 300,000 ounces of gold annually. A conveyer system from the Open Cut carries the ore to the Home- *stake surface plant for processing. Homestake's below-ground operations go as deep as 8,000ft, and the galleries spread out the length and breadth of the Black Hills.*

19-mile-long canyon is blessed with some great scenery and is a favorite ride of visitors to the rally. It also has campsites, fishing, places to eat, and not-too-many people.

The town of Spearfish, at the northern entrance to the canyon, sees many visitors during the course of the rally, yet it somehow manages to remain a quiet haven. It offers camping, plus a number of restaurants, and Sturgis is an easy 18 miles to the southeast on Interstate 90.

Round trip mileage from Sturgis: 60 miles

Time required: Half a day for an easy excursion, easily a good chunk of a day if you want to stretch it

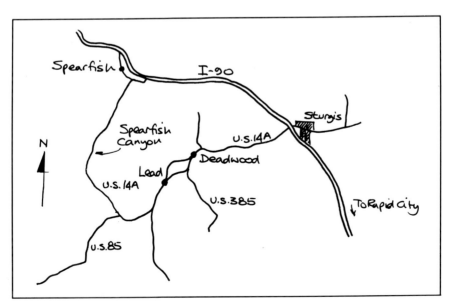

Chapter 6

Old Fort Meade, Custer Monument, and Bear Butte Ride

Sometimes you'll want to cruise Main Street, park the bike, and then cruise Main Street some more, on foot. Everyone does. When you need to get back on the bike and go somewhere, think local. The Old Fort Meade Museum, for instance.

Two miles east of Sturgis on Highway 34, the fort is now for the most part a veterans hospital, but many of the original buildings still remain, and the museum is housed in one of these. Old Fort Meade Museum is well worth your time, if for no other reason than its collection of photographs and artifacts depicting the harshness of a soldier's life in the Black Hills 100 years ago.

Those for whom the word *fort* conjures up the image of an isolated wooden structure out on the prairie should know that Fort Meade doesn't fit the bill at all, and never really did! Perhaps when built in the late eighteen hundreds Fort Meade did have a more isolated look, but by then it seems the U.S. government had abandoned the defensive fort design in favor of a more campus-type ap-

The Old Fort Meade Museum depicts the harshness of military life on the plains 100 years ago. The museum is housed in one of the many buildings that surround Fort Meade's original parade ground.

proach. Despite the setting, life was still hard for the men of the Seventh Cavalry. The winters were cold, the summers hot, and the soldiers were there solely to protect the citizens taking over the Indians' sacred Black Hills in order to strip the streams of gold.

The first commander of Fort Meade was Colonel Samuel D. Sturgis. The colonel gave his name to the town that sprang up 2 miles away, and it was in Sturgis that many of the soldiers had their fun. The town was a little more boisterous back then than it is during rally week today. On Main Street were saloons, gambling, and dance hall girls. The soldiers probably saw more action of one form or another in Sturgis than they ever did out on the plains.

When General George A. Custer came to the Black Hills in 1874 in search of gold, his expedition camped for two nights in the northern hills not far from the site on which Fort Meade was eventually built. The force was 1,200 troopers strong, and the general brought with him many of the comforts of home: a black female cook, champagne, glee clubs, and bands. Because of its size, the expedition required considerable acreage on which to set up camp. The site is marked by a stone monument on the edge of a dirt road. Though it is

Buffalo can be seen in several places in the Black Hills. This herd lives within Bear Butte State Park.

easy to find, few visitors know of its existence.

To find the monument, from Fort Meade, continue east on Highway 34 and turn right at the signs for Buffalo Chip Campground and the airport. Instead of turning immediately left towards Buffalo Chip, take the dirt road south for 2 miles, where you will see the monument to your left.

When you turn off your engine and the only movement is that of the wind gently blowing through the tall grass, you can almost see and hear the sights and sounds of the past.

Square white tents stand in long lines, and troopers on foot and horse-back go about their duties. Some distance away, a herd of cows and goats graze side by side with buffalo. They are watched over by several troopers whose horses stand motionless. A group of mounted officers is taking directions from a photographer who appears from under a black cloth draped over his camera. When the flash powder finally ignites, several horses become skittish and move forward and backward until checked by their riders. To the right, smoke from the wood fires of army kitchens indicates that a meal is being prepared. Sitting in a barber's chair outside a tent not 30 yards away, young General Custer is having his beard trimmed by the expedition's barber.

A charismatic figure, Custer holds court like a king. Seated in a semicircle in front of him, a number of officers strain to catch his every word. There is laughter of the kind that men make when no women are around. It is midafternoon, and to the west, heavy dark clouds signify the advent of an approaching thunderstorm.

"It'll rain for sure." A voice breaks my reverie.

"I'm sorry?" I say.

"I saw you looking at the clouds. The rain, it'll be here by supper time." The voice comes from a guy in his late twenties astride a Fatboy stopped not 5 feet away.

"You live around here?" I ask.

"Nah," he says, "but I've lived in the Midwest long enough to know that there's a storm coming."

We introduce ourselves and talk for a while. He is from a town in Nebraska, works in a local factory, and is on his fourth visit to Sturgis. He also admires the general and is retracing the route of the 1874 expedition through the Black Hills.

"You know," he says as I prepare to leave, "If there had been bikes in Custer's time, he would have ridden a Harley."

It's a long way to the top. The summit of Bear Butte can be reached by a trail that begins above the visitor center in the state park.

60

I had to agree with him.

After retracing your steps to the highway and turning back toward Sturgis, head north on State Highway 79 past the drag strip in the direction of Bear Butte State Park. As state parks go, Bear Butte isn't exactly the largest you will ever visit, but it does contain the one animal everyone expects to see on the plains: the buffalo. Although the mighty beasts can be found in the southern Black Hills and near Devils Tower to the west, Bear Butte State Park is about as close to Sturgis as you will ever see them.

Then there is Bear Butte. Like Devils Tower, it is a leftover from when the earth was young and, in geological parlance, is known as a laccolith. This is a molten core that after forcing its way to the surface, for whatever reason, never quite made it to being a volcano.

Directly behind the park visitor center, Bear Butte beckons the energetic souls who feed on a challenge. Fourteen hundred feet high, the top can be reached by a trail that zigzags back and forth. But perhaps it's time to be returning to Main Street!

The National Motorcycle Museum is located on Junction Avenue, at exit 30, off Interstate 90, in Sturgis. Opened in 1990, the museum is still in its infancy.

Once back in Sturgis, you might want to visit the National Motorcycle Museum on Junction Avenue. The museum has only been open since 1990, so don't expect too much yet. Plans for the future, however, do envisage a much larger collection in a remodeled building.

Round trip mileage from Sturgis: Maximum 20 miles

Time required: 3 hours

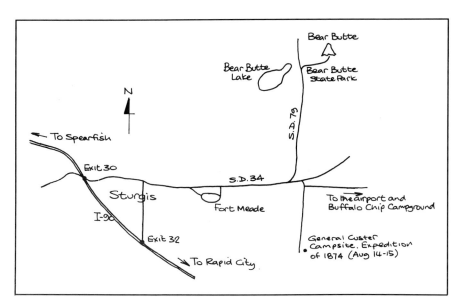

Chapter 7

The Harley-Davidson Traveling Show

It may seem strange that when the vast majority of motorcycles in Sturgis during rally week are Harleys, Harley-Davidson, the company, has very little actual corporate exposure in the town. While someone, somewhere, might be able to twist this fact into something it isn't, the truth is that Sturgis simply doesn't have enough space anywhere for the show Harley-Davidson now puts on in Rapid City every year.

Okay, okay. Someone is about to point out that the Sturgis Fairgrounds are large enough to accommodate Harley-Davidson. Racing is still a big draw in the town, however, and with Harley camped out on the property, there probably wouldn't be much of the fairgrounds track left to race on.

After an extremely rocky start, the eighties were pretty good to Harley-Davidson. The bikes not only looked good, they ran well and attracted more buyers each year. Following the repurchase from American Machine and Foundry (AMF), Harley-Davidson went through tough times, but

the buy-back was a rejuvenation. The company was suddenly young again and began acting as young companies do: designing and packaging innovative products and then going out and selling them. And what better place to show those products than Sturgis, where the overwhelming majority of riders arrive on a Harley. Unfortunately, Sturgis as an event was also growing to where it offered insufficient space to exhibit.

Some people in Sturgis believe the rally will eventually follow Harley-

Sturgis having insufficient available space to consolidate all of its activities into one area, Harley-Davidson moved to the Rapid City civic center. An indoor show highlights all of Harley-Davidson's new models, accessories, and clothes.

With her engaging smile and down-home Texas drawl, Krisann Whitley was a popular Ms. Harley-Davidson.

63

Outside activities include a ride-in show often attracts unusual entries. Some people take the "hog" thing real seriously.

Davidson and move to Rapid City. Rapid City maintains that Sturgis is now simply too small to accommodate the crowds. Obviously, no one knows what changes the future might bring, but it is just too hard to ever envisage referring to the rally as Rapid rather than Sturgis.

Harley-Davidson's best-known ambassador, Willie G. Davidson, always finds time to stop and chat with enthusiasts.

Rushmore Plaza Civic Center, Harley-Davidson's rally headquarters, is easily accessible from exits 57 and 58 off Interstate 90. The facility is a recently built, medium-sized convention center with ample parking and lots of clean toilets.

Throughout rally week, Harley-Davidson–sponsored events and shows occur every day at the civic center. An indoor show features the complete model year line-up; parts, accessories, and collectibles; plus the seemingly ever-expanding line of Harley-Davidson leather clothing. For the fun of it, you might want to attend one of the fashion shows in the theater and then head on over to the retail outlet, where you will find a pretty good assortment of shirts, sweats, and leather looking for a good home.

All Harley Owners Group (HOG) members are invited to participate in events at the center throughout the week. A HOG Hospitality Room is open, so drop on by and learn about the Chapter Challenge, Observation Run, and Ladies of Harley Scavenger Hunt. You can also browse in a HOG merchandise area and receive a free breakfast for showing your HOG card.

Proving that women are the measure of men, Ladies of Harley has its own program, which includes a service seminar, the group's own class at the company's ride-in show, and a Stud Your Duds Workshop. Go to it, ladies!

Since bikers love rock 'n' roll, Harley goes all out to put on a big-name concert. ZZ Top and the Doobie Brothers have appeared to sold-out audiences in the civic center theater, and all proceeds have been donated to the Muscular Dystrophy Foundation.

If the indoor activities can be classified as "company," then the outdoor events are definitely "people."

There's a ride-in bike show, field games, a poker run, live music, vendors, and the Harley-Davidson semitrailer museum. In fact, *something* is going on for most of each day throughout the week.

If you are a Harley-Davidson fan, chances are you'll wander down to Rapid City sometime during the week. Harley's new headquarters is not Sturgis, and neither does it try to be, but it is still fun, and in many ways it is a little pocket of normality in an otherwise crazy week.

Round trip mileage from Sturgis: 58

Time required: Minimum 4 hours

Although most of the Harley-Davidson's presence is in Rapid City, the demo rides are still in Sturgis, next to the Super 8 Motel, at exit 30, off Interstate 90.

Well-known for his Daytona shows, Karl "Big Daddy Rat" Smith finally brought his Rat's Hole Custom Bike Show to Sturgis in 1987.

The antique section at the Rat's Hole Custom Bike Show grows a little larger every year.

Owners have hundreds of hours of work and thousands of dollars invested in the classic custom bike.

Chapter 8

Rat's Hole Custom Bike Show

Karl ("Big Daddy Rat") Smith has been organizing custom bike shows during bike week at Daytona for as long as anyone can remember. In 1987, he brought his Rat's Hole Custom Bike Show to Sturgis and achieved instant success, even though the event was held during a cloudburst. The weather gods have been good to Karl ever since, and a lot of people look forward to Friday of rally week for the show.

In your visits to Main Street, you will no doubt see *some* of the interesting bikes and people in town for the rally. Your chance of seeing them all together in one place, however, is much greater if you go to Sturgis City Park on Friday. Smith's bike show has a way of attracting the best and the bizarre of everything. It's fun; go see it!

Many world-class customs make their way to Sturgis and into the Rat's Hole Custom Bike Show every year.

For some, the elbow grease and polish are applied right up until the time the judges arrive.

Chapter 9

Southern Hills Ride

Not much remains of the old mining town of Rochford, so not too many people go there anymore. But don't let that stop you from making a visit. Ride south from Lead on U.S. Highway 14A/85 and hang a left on County Road 17. Follow 17 until the asphalt gives out, and then it's another couple of miles on gravel to Rochford.

The roads in the Rochford area, mostly gravel, are pretty good, but you can expect to eat a little dust when you meet the occasional car or bike coming from the opposite direction. Look at it this way: *Off the beaten track and hard to get to* translates into "a pleasant ride with very few other tourists and no parking problems" when you arrive. What you get for your effort is one of the best home-cooked meals in South Dakota and an opportunity to visit with Roy and Betsy Harn, owners and operators of the Moonshine Gulch Saloon.

You can't miss the Gulch: it is one of the only buildings still standing in

Crazy Horse Monument, silhouetted on the horizon, was the dream of one man: Sculptor Korczak Ziolkowski. The project is funded solely by a modest entrance fee, and nearly 8 million tons of rock have been removed from the mountain since work started in 1947.

Rochford, and it will draw you like a magnet. Inside, a half-dozen tables with an assortment of chairs cater to a few locals and whatever tourists happen by. The place is decorated with just about everything and anything, but it all seems to work.

And then there's Betsy.

Within 5 minutes, she'll have you feeling as if you are part of the family. She'll eventually get around to taking your order, and Roy, her husband, who tends to stay in the background, will start cooking. She'll probably bring you your first beer or soda, but after that, you'll help yourself from the cooler. You won't mind, of course, because the place has the kind of atmosphere you don't find too much of anymore, with strangers who actually want to talk with you. The result is that a meal at Betsy and Roy's can take a long time.

In 1879, Rochford was a thriving gold-mining town of some 500 people, 200 houses, and a block of stores. It is most remembered for its huge stamp mill, the Stand-by, a picture of which, in its later years with the roof ready to collapse, hangs on the wall of the Gulch.

Leaving Rochford, head east and then south on County Road 231, again gravel, toward Mystic, a momentary stop on the way to Hill City. At the junction of two railroads, Mys-

The Moonshine Gulch Saloon is one of the last remaining buildings in Rochford. Make a point of stopping in.

tic was the site of a large experimental plant that attempted to extract gold from rock by a chlorination process. The plant was a failure, and frequent floods put the Black Hills and Western Railroad out of business. Today, only a sign and two small houses mark the site of this once bustling town.

Approximately 6 miles further south on 231, the gravel ends at Highway 17 which leads to Hill City. Hill City is the terminus of the Black Hills Central Railroad, which operates passenger steam trains to Keystone during the summer months. Needless to say, if you enjoy steam locomotives, this is a mandatory stop.

A few miles south of Hill City on Highway 16/385, you'll find the largest and most ambitious sculpting project in the world: the Crazy Horse Memorial. A tribute to the American Indian, the design features Chief Crazy Horse astride his horse. Much larger than Mount Rushmore the sculpture will take many more years to complete. Begun in 1947 by Sculptor Korczak Ziolkowski, the nonprofit project inches toward completion solely on the money collected from entrance fees.

Crazy Horse is the largest sculptural undertaking in the world. When it is completed, the four presidents' faces on Mount Rushmore will fit into the space occupied by Chief Crazy Horse's head. The entrance to Crazy Horse is through gates containing brass silhouettes of 270 birds, animals, plants, and trees found in the Black Hills. The gates were designed by Korczak Ziolkowski and built by his family. Since Ziolkowski's death in 1982, his wife, Ruth, and their family have kept up his work on the mountain. Ziolkowski left detailed plans for continuing the piece.

The enormity of what is going on here, and what has been going on here over the years, is worth your stopping by.

After continuing south on Highway 16/385 to Custer, the most southern town on your ride, head east for 2 miles on Highway 16 to French Creek, the place that forever changed the Black Hills. It was here that one H. N. Ross, a member of Custer's expedition of 1874, discovered the gold that began the last American gold rush.

It is a short ride on Highway 16 into Custer State Park, from where you will turn north onto Needles Highway to start the return leg of your journey. Fourteen miles long, Needles Highway was built solely for the views it offers the tourist, and the name comes from tall, pointed granite columns that reach skyward. The vistas are especially spectacular in the late-afternoon sun; be sure to stop and enjoy them. When you reach Sylvan Lake, the end of Needles Highway, return to Sturgis via U.S. Highways 385 and 14A. For an alternate route you might want to try Highway 244 past Mount Rushmore to Keystone, then Highway 16 to

Needles Highway, named for the tall columns of granite along its route, is a 14-mile drive with spectacular views of the southern hills.

Rapid City, and the Interstate to Sturgis.

Round trip mileage from Sturgis: About 180 miles

Time required: All day

A single-lane tunnel on Needles Highway.

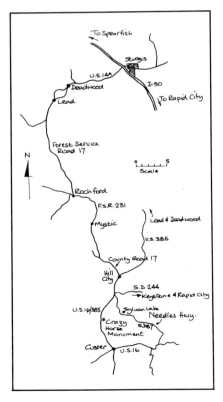

For women, Main Street is not Mean Street.

The kids don't prevent this modern mom from riding; she just loads them on board, where she can keep an eye on them.

Marla Garber rides from Winnipeg, Canada, to Sturgis each year with her trusty companion—Skooter.

Chapter 10

Women on Bikes

They've gone out to work to help pay the mortgage and everything else from food to children's clothing to bike parts. And all the while, they've continued to take care of the kids, do the grocery shopping, prepare meals, and keep the house clean. Our wives, lovers, girlfriends, and significant others—God bless them!

Of course, we men have helped here and there, but most of us haven't had two careers running concurrently—the second one starting when the front door closes, either on the way in or on the way out.

Well, over a period of time, things just naturally change. In addition to getting us to help more with the marketing, the kids, and the housework, women, trained in business skills that emphasize time management and with a couple of bucks in their pocket, are now buying motorcycles and *riding* them. On their own! By themselves! Solo!

In the early eighties, a woman on a motorcycle riding down Main Street would have been the exception to the rule. Today, while not quite the rule, their numbers have increased dramatically. Even Harley-Davidson now recognizes the buying power of women and tailors products to them; women also have a number of clubs, and even a national magazine—*Harley Women*—which has a tremendous following among both women and men. In fact, the first real indication of how many women rode to Sturgis was a Ladies Day organized by *Harley Women* magazine at Hog Heaven Campground in 1989. More than 300 women on bikes attended, and many brought a husband or boyfriend along, too. Boy, times they are a changing!

During the 1989 rally, 300 women participated in the Harley Women *Magazine Ladies Day Ride.*

The motorcycles of choice for most junior racers are the Woods Rotax and Harley-Davidson. Both machines use the Austrian single-cylinder 600cc Rotax engine.

Experts ride the Harley-Davidson XR750 and the Honda RS750. Both are 750cc V-twins that can make in excess of 90 horsepower.

Chapter 11

Racing

Racing has been a part of the Sturgis rally since Sturgis resident J.C. "Pappy" Hoel came up with the idea of a two-day rally and racing get-together back in 1938. The rally and races were a much simpler affair back then, and many of the bikes ridden to the rally were stripped down for the races, then rebuilt to ride home. Hoel, a member of the Jackpine Gypsies Motorcycle Club, lived many years to see the classic become a huge success, but he was the first to admit that he never for one moment envisaged anything on such a grand scale.

As the rally has grown, so has the race program. Six different kinds of racing now take place throughout the week. The Black Hills Speedway in ..pid City and the fairgrounds in ... ld AMA (American Motor- .. sociation) national and re- ,..nal half-mile dirt track events for the guys—and occasionally gals—who make their living racing motorcycles. Vintage dirt track racing has also been added to the schedule at the fairgrounds. To qualify, vintage bikes must have been built before 1975. Not unexpectedly, vintage bike riders are also a little long in the tooth, but if they've lost some of their former edge, most make it up in cunning!

Across the freeway from the Sturgis Fairgrounds are short track events and a vintage TT (Tourist Trophy) at the Jackpine Gypsies Club Grounds. Friday night, the real big night at the club grounds, is when the top AMA professional riders drop by for a 600 short track national. You can see all the short track action from the grandstand, and typically, the racing takes place at night under the lights. The vintage TT is run on a course adjacent to the short track.

In the same area as the short track and TT is the hill climb. It's not the steepest hill you'll ever see, but it probably is the most dusty. To truly enjoy the hill climb, make sure you are upwind of the track.

Without doubt, the racing that draws the largest crowds is the All Harley Drags held at the Sturgis Dragway. Races are held every day throughout the week, including classes for street bikes, but everyone is really there to see the pros ride the nitro- and gas-powered bikes, which hurt the ears and shake the ground. Check them out!

Although it is always subject to change, the rally week race schedule usually sticks to the following outline:

The All-Harley Drag Racing Association series is extremely popular with the spectators.

Monday

Time	Event	Venue
1:00pm	Vintage TT Races	Jackpine Gypsies Club Grounds

Tuesday

Time	Event	Venue
1:30pm	Vintage Half Mile Races	Sturgis Fairgrounds
6:00pm	AHDRA Sturgis King of the Hill	Sturgis Dragway

Action at the drag strip starts in midafternoon and goes on well into the night.

	Drag Racing, Street Class Competition	
7:00pm	AMA Pro-Am Short Track (no amateurs)	Jackpine Gypsies Club Grounds

Wednesday

Time	Event	Venue
10:00am	Vintage Half Mile Races, Vintage "Grudge" Races	Sturgis Fairgrounds
1:00pm	Queen of the Hills Drag Races	Dakota Dragway, Belle Fourche
6:00pm	AHDRA Drag Racing, Pro Qualifying	Sturgis Dragway
7:00pm	Camel Pro AMA 600 National Half Mile Races	Black Hills Speedway, Rapid City
	AMA Pro-Am Short Track, Amateur Night	Jackpine Gypsies Club Grounds

Thursday

Time	Event	Venue
11:00am	AMA Amateur Hill Climb	Jackpine Gypsies Club Grounds
1:00pm	Vintage National Half Mile Races	Sturgis Fairgrounds
3:00pm	AHDRA Sturgis All Harley Drag Nationals, Last-Chance Qualifying	Sturgis Dragway
6:00pm	AHDRA Sturgis All Harley Drag Nationals, Eliminations	Sturgis Dragway
7:00pm	AMA Pro-Am Short Track Races (no amateurs)	Jackpine Gypsies Clubgrounds

Friday

Time	Event	Venue
1:00pm	Vintage Half Mile Nationals Races	Sturgis Fairgrounds
6:00pm	All Harley Drag Racing East versus West Ultimate Harley Showdown	Sturgis Dragway
7:30pm	AMA 600 National Short Track Races	Jackpine Gypsies Club Grounds

Saturday

Time	Event	Venue
1:00pm	AMA Pro-Am Half Mile Races	Sturgis Fairgrounds

Sunday

Time	Event	Venue
1:00pm	AMA Western Regional Championship Half Mile Races	Sturgis Fairgrounds

Chapter 12

Eastern Ride: Ellsworth AFB, Wall Drug, and the Badlands

With all the great scenery in the Black Hills, it might appear unusual to suggest riding east onto the vast expanse of the American prairie. After all, what is there to see out there except a lot of almost treeless rolling land that seems to go on forever? Well, there's a lot more than you might imagine, and the first stop is just east of Rapid City.

Ellsworth Air Force Base is an operational B-1 bomber base that permits public tours on a daily basis. Besides offering static aircraft displays from World War II right on up to a B-52 bomber, Ellsworth is somewhat unique in that visitors can board a bus for a tour of the flight line. Okay, so a chain link fence separates you from the B-1s and the guards don't like you getting real close to the fence; nevertheless, you can watch and take photographs of the big, flat-black–painted bombers being prepared for flight. Ellsworth is at exit 66 off Interstate 90; just follow the signs to the main gate. Admission is free.

Continuing east on Interstate 90, the next stop is the town of Wall, home of Wall Drug. Just over 50 miles from Rapid City, Wall Drug is

This retired B-52 bomber has become part of Ellsworth AFB's static-airplane display.

an oasis on the South Dakota prairie, and achieved its fame by being just that to travelers.

In a Wall Drug brochure, Ted Hustead relates how he and wife Dorothy began offering free ice water to motorists as an inducement to stop at their store. That was back in the thirties, and over the years, Wall Drug has grown to be tremendously successful. The store is now almost a shopping mall, with many different types of shops operating beneath its umbrella, but all remain in the family and retain a distinctly midwestern flavor. And the free ice water is still available.

Wall itself has had to learn to live with success, for at first glance it seems that the town is one giant parking lot for cars and tour buses. But although many of the 20,000 daily visitors might have to look around for a parking space, bikes park easily on Main Street, just steps away from Wall Drug and the other tourist stores.

It is only minutes from Wall south on State Highway 240 to Badlands National Park. This area was once part of a large saltwater sea. Millions of years ago, the water drained away and left marshland. The marshland was fed by rivers, which over time, and along with the wind, eroded away the sedimentary deposits. What

A B-1 bomber is readied for flight at Ellsworth AFB. The ride by bus to the flight line is courtesy of the U.S. Air Force.

Free ice water was the lure Ted and Dorothy Hustead used to get thirsty travelers off the highway and into their Wall drugstore. They've been coming ever since the Depression, in greater numbers each year.

Even though the Badlands appear to live up to their name, an abundance of wild- *life, including buffalo and deer, can be found here.*

is left are canyons and spires plus lots of layered color. Mineral deposits are responsible for the bands of color. The Badlands are also a rich source of fossils, some as old as 25 million years. Remains of animals resembling camels, crocodiles, and three-toed miniature horses have been found there.

When you reach Cedar Pass Visitor Center in the Badlands, you have two options for returning to Rapid City and Sturgis: either Interstate 90 to the north or State Highway 44 to the south. Definitely the lonelier route of the two, Highway 44 parallels the northern edge of the Pine Ridge Indian Reservation and passes through rich grasslands that support cattle and sheep. For 40 miles, you'll be able to count the number of cars, pickup trucks, and bikes on the fingers of one hand. Enjoy the ride.

Approximate round trip mileage from Sturgis: 200

Time required: All day

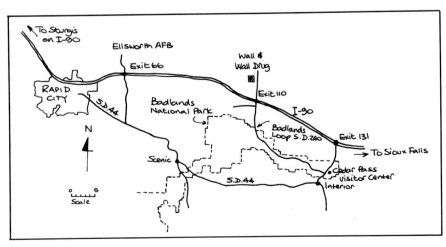

Chapter 13

Mount Rushmore Ride

No visit to Sturgis and the Black Hills would be complete without a ride to Mount Rushmore. You have seen it in photographs, in movies, and on TV, but nothing compares to actually being there and viewing the sculptures for yourself. Don't feel embarrassed if you get a lump in your throat, because the monument has a way of doing that to people.

Mount Rushmore was authorized by an act of Congress on March 4, 1925, that issued a mandate "to carve a memorial of historic figures." Gutzon Borglum, the son of Danish immigrants, was honored with the contract to sculpt the faces, and work started in late 1927. Gutzon died in 1941 before the sculptures were finished, but they were completed by his son, Lincoln. The sculptures are an engineering masterpiece. Although they do not seem to be out of place on the mountain, they are nevertheless massive: the 60-foot-high faces would sit on the shoulders of men 465 feet tall if full statues were done to the same scale.

Sculptor Gutzon Borglum said he wanted the Mount Rushmore memorial high enough "so it will not pay future generations to pull down what we will put up there."

Much of how the work was achieved is documented in photographs at the visitor center, but not much is said about the maintenance work that must be done on the faces. Natural cracks in the granite must be periodically sealed to prevent any moisture from freezing and expanding; expansion could break off pieces of the granite. Access to the faces for repair workers is by bosun's chair from the top; this is the same method used by the construction crews who carved the statues. Gutzon originally ordered the cracks sealed, and his recipe—white lead, linseed oil, and granite dust—has not been improved upon. Geologists have estimated that with care, the sculptures will last 500,000 years. This should be more than ample time for many of your descendants to visit the rally and take the same ride up to Mount Rushmore.

On the way back down from Mount Rushmore you may want to check out Iron Mountain Road (Highway 16A) and the series of wooden "pigtail" bridges which allow the road to climb steeply in a confined space. A few miles further along the road are narrow tunnels, one of which offers perfect framing of Mount Rushmore. A photograph here will impress your friends back home.

Retrace your steps to Keystone for the ride back to Sturgis.

Early morning, when the sun shines directly on the four presidents, is a good time to photograph Mount Rushmore.

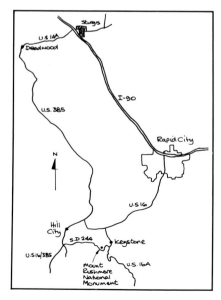

A boom town during the gold rush, Keystone was also the base camp for the men who worked on Mount Rushmore. Today, it caters to the tourist trade with lots of places to eat, museum and mine tours, horseback riding, helicopter tours of Mount Rushmore, a steam train ride to Hill City, an aerial tramway, and a 100-year-old saloon. Chances are you'll stop in Keystone either on the way up to or down from Mount Rushmore.

Round trip mileage from Sturgis: About 100 miles

Time required: At least half a day, more if you want to explore some of the great scenery in the Rushmore area

Sturgis at a Glance

Location
28 miles northwest of Rapid City, South Dakota
425 miles north of Denver, Colorado
675 miles west of Minneapolis, Minnesota

Average Elevation
3,450ft

Distance to Nearby Attractions

Attraction	Miles to Sturgis
Deadwood, SD	12
Spearfish, SD	17
Crazy Horse Memorial, SD	55
Mt. Rushmore, SD	55
Custer State Park, SD	60
Badlands, SD	80
Devils Tower, WY	80

Population
Sturgis, 1990: 5,800 estimated
Sturgis 25-mile radius, 1990: 48,929 estimated

Climate
Average temperature, August: 71.7 degrees Fahrenheit
Average annual precipitation: 17.51 inches
Average annual snowfall: 38.8 inches
Prevailing winds: Northwest

Nearest Airport
Sturgis Municipal
Distance from downtown Sturgis: 6 miles
Runway: 4,600 feet, asphaltic concrete

Commercial Air Service
Rapid City Regional Airport
Distance from downtown Sturgis: 38 miles
Service:
United Express to Denver hub
Delta to Salt Lake City hub
Continental Express to Denver hub
Northwest to Minneapolis hub

Rental Car Companies
Location: Rapid City Regional Airport
Distance from downtown Sturgis: 38 miles
Agencies:
Hertz
Avis
Dollar
Budget
Thrifty

Bus Service
Intracity routes: None
Tours:
Deadwood Stage Bus Tours—Tours originate in Sturgis, Deadwood, and Spearfish, with free pickup service
Jack Rabbit Lines—Tours originate in Rapid City
Gray Line of the Black Hills—Tours originate in Rapid City

Railroad Service
Intracity routes: None

Useful Phone Numbers

Attorneys (Sturgis)
Hansen and Hubbard Law Office
347-2551

Jackley and Flint, Attorneys at Law
347-4592

Morman Law Firm
347-3624

Chambers of Commerce
Custer Chamber of Commerce
(800)992-9818

Hill City Chamber of Commerce
(800)888-1798

Keystone Chamber of Commerce
(800)843-1300, ext. 939

Sturgis Chamber of Commerce
Information Center
(605)347-2556

Spearfish Chamber of Commerce
(800)626-8013

Wall Chamber of Commerce
(605)279-2665

Sturgis Chamber of Commerce
Information Center
(605)347-2556

Chiropractors (Sturgis)
James Sabo
347-5743

Mark Zeigler
347-3535

County Courthouses
Deadwood
Lawrence County Courthouse
   Circuit judge: 578-2044
   County jail: 578-2230
   Court clerk: 578-2040
   Magistrate: 578-2041
   State attorney: 578-1707

Rapid City
Pennington County Courthouse
   Circuit judge: 395-2571
   County jail: 394-6116
   Court clerk: 394-2575
   Detoxification: 394-6128
   Magistrate: 394-2570
   Sheriff: 394-2151
   State attorney: 394-6117

Sturgis
Meade County Courthouse
   Circuit judge: 347-4413
   Court clerk: 347-4411
   Magistrate: 347-4409
   Sheriff: 347-2681
   State attorney: 347-4491

Dentists (Sturgis)
Donald Bachand
347-3373

Walter Raymond
347-2660

Rick Schmid
347-5103

Fire Departments
Belle Fourche
892-2737

Deadwood
578-1212

Ft. Meade
347-2200

Lead
584-1313

Piedmont
394-4135

Rapid City
911

Sturgis
347-3611

General Information
Alcohol Referral Center (Sturgis)
347-3003

Alcoholics Anonymous (Sturgis)
347-9909

Ambulance service (Sturgis)
347-2573

Ellsworth AFB
385-1000

National Weather Service
393-1431

Road Conditions
394-2255 or 394-2243

Western Land Brokers (pick up or
send money)
347-5000

Western Union
(800)325-6000

Women in Crisis (domestic abuse)
    Belle Fourche: 892-4192
    Deadwood: 578-2405
    Rapid City: 341-4808
    Spearfish: 642-7825
    Sturgis: 347-2573 (police)

Highway Patrol
Deadwood-Lead
578-2230

Rapid City
394-2286

Hospitals
Belle Fourche
Belle Fourche Health Care Center
2200 13th Ave.
892-3331

Custer
Custer Community Hospital
1039 Montgomery St.
673-2229

Deadwood
Northern Hills General Hospital
61 Charles St.
578-2313

Ellsworth AFB
Ellsworth AFB Hospital
I-90, exit 66
385-3430

Ft. Meade
Ft. Meade Veterans' Administration
(VA) Medical Center
3 miles east of Sturgis on Hwys. 34
and 79
347-2511

Hot Springs
Hot Springs VA Medical Center
Hot Springs 745-2000

Southern Hills General Hospital
209 N. 16th St.
745-3159

Rapid City
Black Hills Rehabilitation Hospital
2908 5th St.
399-1111

Rapid City Regional Hospital
353 Fairmont Blvd.
341-1000

Spearfish
Lookout Memorial Hospital
1440 N. Main
642-2617

Sturgis
Sturgis Community Health Care
Center
949 Harmon St.
347-2536

Medical Clinics
Custer
Custer Clinic
1041 Montgomery St.
673-2201

Deadwood
Black Hills Medical Center PC
71 Charles St.
578-2364

New Horizons Alcohol/Drug
Dependency
61 Charles St.
578-2313

Hot Springs
Black Hills Clinic PC
130 N. 15th St.
745-6100

Piedmont
Piedmont Medical Center
Stagebarn Canyon Rd.
787-6714

Rapid City
Black Hills Eye Institute
2800 S. 3rd St.
341-2000

Black Hills Pediatrics
2929 S. 5th St.
341-7337

Dermatology Clinic
717 Meade
348-4410

Rapid Care Medical Center
I-90 at Haines
341-6600

Rapid City Medical Center
728 Columbus St.
342-3280

Spearfish
Family Medical Center
1406 Main St.
642-4648

Sturgis
Massa Berry Professional
Association
981 Main St.
347-3616

Psychological Association
981 Main St.
347-5000

Sturgis Medical Center
1010 Ball Park Rd.
347-3684

Optometrist (Sturgis)
Hines, Watson, Prosser
347-2666

Poison Control Centers
Rapid City: 341-3333
South Dakota: (800)952-0123

Police
Deadwood
578-2345

Lead
584-1722

Sturgis
347-2573

Veterinarians (Sturgis)
John A. Ismay
347-4436

Johnson and Jones
347-3606

John Raforth
347-2890

Appendix C

Calendar of Rally Events

The rally attracts big name artists to concerts at Rapid City civic center theater, Buffalo Chip Campground, and Bentshoe, a relatively new location in Sturgis. Performers have included: Willie Nelson and Waylon Jennings, The Doobie Brothers, ZZ Top, John Kay and Steppenwolf, Charlie Daniels Band, Eric Burdon, The Marshall Tucker Band, and Johnny Paycheck. Many bands return on a regular basis and no one leaves a rally concert admitting to not having a good time. The campground concerts in Sturgis are turn up and pay at the gate affairs, but because of the limited seating you'll need to buy tickets in advance of Harley's Rapid City Concert.

Buffalo Chip is also known for its practically nonstop entertainment throughout rally week, not all of which is provided by the management. If you like to party check out Buffalo Chip.

In past years the following events have been part of Sturgis rally week. There may be others that we don't know of, and some that have been added, replaced or rescheduled at different times. So, before heading to any particular event take a moment to check actual date, time and location.

A night on Main Street should be on everyone's calendar of events.

Sunday

Time	Event	Venue
10:00am–6:00pm	Vintage and Indian Motorcycle Convention, Sign-in Vintage Motorcycle Swap Meet, Setup	Sturgis Fairgrounds
9:00pm	Concert	Buffalo Chip Campground, Sturgis

Monday

Time	Event	Venue
9:00am–3:00pm	Harley-Davidson Demo Rides	Super 8 Motel, Sturgis
9:00am–6:00pm	Run for the Gold Poker Run, Preregistration	Black Hills Harley-Davidson, Rapid City
10:00am	Vintage and Indian Motorcycle Convention, Opening Ceremonies and Recognition Day	Sturgis Fairgrounds
10:00am–4:00pm	Vintage Motorcycle Swap Meet	Sturgis Fairgrounds
1:00pm	British Bikes Field Meet	Sturgis Fairgrounds
	Vintage TT Races	Jackpine Gypsies Club Grounds, Sturgis
4:00pm–7:00pm	Harley-Davidson Welcome Reception	Rushmore Plaza Civic Center Parking Lot, Rapid City
9:00pm	Concert	Buffalo Chip Campground, Sturgis

Tuesday

Time	Event	Venue
9:00am	Northern Hills Tour to Devils Tower, Departure	City auditorium, Sturgis
9:00am–3:00pm	Harley-Davidson Demo Rides	Super 8 Motel, Sturgis
9:00am–6:00pm	Run for the Gold Poker Run, Preregistration	Black Hills Harley-Davidson, Rapid City
9:30am	Vintage and Indian Motorcycle Convention	Sturgis Fairgrounds
10:00am	Black Hills HOG Chapter Tour of the Black Hills (HOG members and their guests only)	Rushmore Plaza Civic Center, Rapid City
	Vintage Bikes 60-Mile Black Hills Tour	Sturgis Fairgrounds
10:00am–4:00pm	Vintage Motorcycle Swap Meet	Sturgis Fairgrounds
12:00pm	Indian and Vintage Motorcycle Parade	Sturgis Fairgrounds
12:00pm–6:00pm	Harley-Davidson Indoor Show: HOG merchandise, Harley-Davidson Sturgis T-shirt sales, dealer retail outlet, HOG hospitality (Chapter	Rushmore Plaza Civic Center, Rapid City

	Challenge, Observation Run, Ladies of Harley Scavenger Hunt)	
	Harley-Davidson Outdoor Show: Harley-Davidson Travelling Museum, HOG Mall, outside entertainment	Rushmore Plaza Civic Center, Rapid City
1:30pm	Vintage Half Mile Races	Sturgis Fairgrounds
2:00pm–4:00pm	Harley-Davidson Service Seminar	Rushmore Plaza Civic Center, Rapid City
3:00pm	AHDRA Sturgis King of the Hill Street Class Competition, Gates Open	Sturgis Dragway
6:00pm	AHDRA Sturgis King of the Hill Street Class Competition, Eliminations	Sturgis Dragway
6:00pm–9:00pm	Vintage and Classic Motorcycle Auction, Preview	Sturgis Junior High School Gymnasium
7:00pm	AMA Pro-Am Short Track Races (no amateurs)	Jackpine Gypsies Club Grounds, Sturgis
8:00pm	Harley-Davidson Concert (reserved seating only)	Rushmore Plaza Civic Center, Rapid City
9:00pm	Concert	Buffalo Chip Campground, Sturgis

Wednesday

Time	Event	Venue
9:00am	Southern Hills Tour to Mt. Rushmore, Departure	City auditorium, Sturgis
8:00am–6:00pm	Run for the Gold Poker Run	Rushmore Plaza Civic Center Parking Lot, Rapid City
9:00am	Vintage and Indian Motorcycle Convention	Sturgis Fairgrounds
9:00am–3:00pm	Harley-Davidson Demo Rides	Super 8 Motel, Sturgis
10:00am	Vintage Half Mile Races, Vintage "Grudge" Races	Sturgis Fairgrounds
	Vintage and Classic Motorcycle Auction	Sturgis Junior High School Gymnasium
10:00am–4:00pm	Vintage Motorcycle Swap Meet	Sturgis Fairgrounds
10:00am–6:00pm	Harley-Davidson and HOG activities (see Tuesday, 12:00pm–6:00pm)	Rushmore Plaza Civic Center, Rapid City
10:30am–12:00pm	Motorcycle Rights Organization Breakfast Buffet	Holiday Inn, Spearfish
11:00am–1:00pm	Harley-Davidson Service Seminar	Rushmore Plaza Civic Center, Rapid City
12:00pm	Motorcycle Rights Organization Meeting	Holiday Inn, Spearfish

Time	Event	Venue
1:00pm	Queen of the Hills Drag Races	Dakota Dragway, Belle Fourche
1:00pm–3:00pm	Ladies of Harley Stud Your Duds Workshop	Rushmore Plaza Civic Center, Rapid City
2:00pm	Vintage Harley-Davidson Tribute; Vintage Motorcycle Parade	Sturgis Fairgrounds
2:00pm–4:00pm	Harley-Davidson Service Seminar	Rushmore Plaza Civic Center, Rapid City
3:00pm	AHDRA Pro Qualifying, Gates Open	Sturgis Dragway
4:00pm–6:00pm	HOG Chapter Officer Reception	Rushmore Plaza Civic Center, Rapid City
6:00pm	AHDRA Pro Qualifying Eliminations	Sturgis Dragway
7:00pm	Camel Pro AMA 600 National Half Mile Races	Black Hills Speedway, Rapid City
	AMA Pro-Am Short Track, Amateur Night	Jackpine Gypsies Club Grounds, Sturgis
9:00pm	Concert	Buffalo Chip Campground, Sturgis

Thursday

Time	Event	Venue
8:00am–11:00am	Harley-Davidson Ride-in Show, Registration	Rushmore Plaza Civic Center Parking Lot, Rapid City
9:00am	Vintage and Indian Motorcycle Convention	Sturgis Fairgrounds
9:00am–3:00pm	Harley-Davidson Demo Rides	Super 8 Motel, Sturgis
	Harley-Davidson Ride-in Show	Rushmore Plaza Civic Center Parking Lot, Rapid City
10:00am–4:00pm	Vintage Motorcycle Swap Meet	Sturgis Fairgrounds
	Annual *Harley Women* Magazine Ladies Day	Hog Heaven Campground, Sturgis
10:00am–6:00pm	Harley-Davidson and HOG activities (see Tuesday, 12:00pm–6:00pm)	Rushmore Plaza Civic Center, Rapid City
10:30am	Annual Zodiac Angels Black Hills Ladies Run to Hill City, and Rodeo,	Departure: Lynn's County Market, Sturgis
11:00am	AMA Amateur Hill Climb	Jackpine Gypsies Club Grounds, Sturgis
11:00am–1:00pm	Ladies of Harley Service Seminar	Rushmore Plaza Civic Center, Rapid City
1:00pm	Vintage National Half Mile Races	Sturgis Fairgrounds
2:00pm	Vintage Motorcycle Parade	Sturgis Fairgrounds
	MotorClothes Fashion Show	Rushmore Plaza Civic

Time	Event	Venue
		Center Theater, Rapid City
2:00pm–4:00pm	Harley-Davidson Service Seminar	Rushmore Plaza Civic Center, Rapid City
3:00pm	AHDRA Sturgis All Harley Drag Nationals, Last-Chance Qualifying	Sturgis Dragway
6:00pm	AHDRA Sturgis All Harley Drag Nationals, Eliminations	Sturgis Dragway
7:00pm	AMA Pro-Am Short Track Races (no amateurs)	Jackpine Gypsies Club Grounds, Sturgis
9:00pm	Concert	Buffalo Chip Campground, Sturgis

Friday

Time	Event	Venue
7:30am–8:30am	Rat's Hole Custom Chopper Show, Contestants' Entry	Sturgis City Park
8:00am–10:00am	HOG Breakfast (members only)	Hall D, Rushmore Plaza Civic Center, Rapid City
9:00am	Vintage and Indian Motorcycle Convention	Sturgis Fairgrounds
	Rat's Hole Custom Chopper Show, Gates Open	Sturgis City Park
9:00am–3:00pm	Harley-Davidson Demo Rides	Super 8 Motel, Sturgis
10:00am–4:00pm	Vintage Motorcycle Swap Meet	Sturgis Fairgrounds
10:00am–6:00pm	Harley-Davidson and HOG activities (see Tuesday, 12:00pm–6:00pm)	Rushmore Plaza Civic Center, Rapid City
11:00am–1:00pm	Harley-Davidson Service Seminar	Rushmore Plaza Civic Center, Rapid City
11:00am–2:00pm	Harley-Davidson Field Events	Rushmore Plaza Civic Center Parking Lot, Rapid City
1:00pm	Vintage Half-Mile National Races	Sturgis Fairgrounds
2:00pm	MotorClothes Fashion Show	Rushmore Plaza Civic Center Theater, Rapid City
	Vintage Motorcycle Parade	Sturgis Fairgrounds
2:00pm–4:00pm	Harley-Davidson Service Seminar	Rushmore Plaza Civic Center, Rapid City
3:00pm	Ladies of Harley Group Photograph	Rushmore Plaza Civic Center Parking Lot, Rapid City
	AHDRA East versus West Ultimate Harley Showdown, Gates Open	Sturgis Dragway
4:30pm	Vintage and Indian Motorcycle Convention, Closing Ceremonies and Trophy	Sturgis Fairgrounds

	Presentations	
5:00pm	Rat's Hole Custom Chopper Show; Motorcycle Riders Foundation Raffle for Harley-Davidson Motorcycle	Sturgis Park
6:00pm	AHDRA East versus West Ultimate Harley Showdown, Eliminations	Sturgis Dragway
7:00pm	AMA 600 National Short Track Races	Jackpine Gypsies Club Grounds, Sturgis
9:00pm	Concert	Buffalo Chip Campground, Sturgis

Saturday

Time	Event	Venue
9:00am–3:00pm	Harley-Davidson Demo Rides	Super 8 Motel, Sturgis
10:00am–4:00pm	Harley-Davidson and HOG activities (see Tuesday, 12:00pm–6:00pm)	Rushmore Plaza Civic Center, Rapid City
11:00am–1:00pm	Harley-Davidson Service Seminar	Rushmore Plaza Civic Center, Rapid City
12:00pm	Motorcycle Riders Foundation Raffle for Harley-Davidson Motorcycle	Rushmore Plaza Civic Center, Rapid City
1:00pm	AMA Pro-Am Half Mile Races Sturgis Fairgrounds	2:00pm–4:00pm
Harley-Davidson Service Seminar	Rushmore Plaza Civic Center, Rapid City	9:00pm
Concert	Buffalo Chip Campground, Sturgis	

Sunday

Time	Event	Venue
1:00pm	AMA Western Regional Championship Half Mile Races	Sturgis Fairgrounds